Gerald P. Mallon,
Editor

Social Services
with Transgendered Youth

Social Services with Transgendered Youth has been co-published simultaneously as *Journal of Gay & Lesbian Social Services*, Volume 10, Numbers 3/4 1999.

Social Services
with Transgendered Youth

Social Services with Transgendered Youth has been co-published simultaneously as *Journal of Gay & Lesbian Social Services,* Volume 10, Numbers 3/4 1999.

The *Journal of Gay & Lesbian Social Services* Monographic "Separates"

Below is a list of "separates," which in serials librarianship means a special issue simultaneously published as a special journal issue or double-issue *and* as a "separate" hardbound monograph. (This is a format which we also call a "DocuSerial.")

"Separates" are published because specialized libraries or professionals may wish to purchase a specific thematic issue by itself in a format which can be separately cataloged and shelved, as opposed to purchasing the journal on an on-going basis. Faculty members may also more easily consider a "separate" for classroom adoption.

"Separates" are carefully classified separately with the major book jobbers so that the journal tie-in can be noted on new book order slips to avoid duplicate purchasing.

You may wish to visit Haworth's Website at . . .

http://www.haworthpressinc.com

. . . to search our online catalog for complete tables of contents of these separates and related publications.

You may also call 1-800-HAWORTH (outside US/Canada: 607-722-5857), or Fax 1-800-895-0582 (outside US/Canada: 607-771-0012), or e-mail at:

getinfo@haworthpressinc.com

Social Services with Transgendered Youth, edited by Gerald P. Mallon, DSW (Vol. 10, No. 3/4, 1999). *"A well-articulated book that provides valuable information about a population that has been virtually ignored. . . ." (Carol T. Tully, PhD, Associate Professor, Tulane University, School of Social Work, New Orleans, Louisiana)*

Queer Families, Common Agendas: Gay People, Lesbians, and Family Values, edited by T. Richard Sullivan, PhD (Vol. 10, No. 1, 1999). *Examines the real life experience of those affected by current laws and policies regarding homosexual families.*

Lady Boys, Tom Boys, Rent Boys: Male and Female Homosexualities in Contemporary Thailand, edited by Peter A. Jackson, PhD, and Gerard Sullivan, PhD (Vol. 9, No. 2/3, 1999). *"Brings to life issues and problems of interpreting sexual and gender identities in contemporary Thailand." (Nerida M. Cook, PhD, Lecturer in Sociology, Department of Sociology and Social Work, University of Tasmania, Australia)*

Working with Gay Men and Lesbians in Private Psychotherapy Practice, edited by Christopher J. Alexander, PhD (Vol. 8, No. 4, 1998). *"Rich with information that will prove especially invaluable to therapists planning to or recently having begun to work with lesbian and gay clients in private practice." (Michael Shernoff, MSW, Private Practice, NYC; Adjunct Faculty, Hunter College Graduate School of Social Work)*

Violence and Social Injustice Against Lesbian, Gay and Bisexual People, edited by Lacey M. Sloan, PhD, and Nora S. Gustavsson, PhD (Vol. 8, No. 3, 1998). *"An important and timely book that exposes the multilevel nature of violence against gay, lesbian, bisexual, and transgender people." (Dorothy Van Soest, DSW, Associate Dean, School of Social Work, University of Texas at Austin)*

The HIV-Negative Gay Man: Developing Strategies for Survival and Emotional Well-Being, edited by Steven Ball, MSW, ACSW (Vol. 8, No. 1, 1998). *"Essential reading for anyone working with HIV-negative gay men." (Walt Odets, PhD, Author, In the Shadow of the Epidemic: Being HIV-Negative in the Age of AIDS; Clinical Psychologist, private practice, Berkeley, California)*

School Experiences of Gay and Lesbian Youth: The Invisible Minority, edited by Mary B. Harris, PhD (Vol. 7, No. 4, 1998). *"Our schools are well served when authors such as these have the courage to highlight problems that schools deny and to advocate for students whom schools make invisible." (Gerald Unks, Professor, School of Education, University of North Carolina at Chapel Hill; Editor, The Gay Teen.) Provides schools with helpful suggestions for becoming places that welcome gay and lesbian students and, therefore, better serve the needs of all students.*

Rural Gays and Lesbians: Building on the Strengths of Communities, edited by James Donald Smith, ACSW, LCSW, and Ronald J. Mancoske, BSCW, DSW (Vol. 7, No. 3, 1998). *"This informative and well-written book fills a major gap in the literature and should be widely read." (James Midgley, PhD, Harry and Riva Specht Professor of Public Social Services and Dean, School of Social Welfare, University of California at Berkeley)*

Gay Widowers: Life After the Death of a Partner, edited by Michael Shernoff, MSW, ACSW (Vol. 7, No. 2, 1997). *"This inspiring book is not only for those who have experienced the tragedy of losing a partner–it's for every gay man who loves another." (Michelangelo Signorile, author, Life Outside)*

Gay and Lesbian Professionals in the Closet: Who's In, Who's Out, and Why, edited by Teresa DeCrescenzo, MSW, LCSW (Vol. 6, No. 4, 1997). *"A gripping example of the way the closet cripples us and those we try to serve." (Virginia Uribe, PhD, Founder, Project 10 Outreach to Gay and Lesbian Youth, Los Angeles Unified School District)*

Two Spirit People: American Indian Lesbian Women and Gay Men, edited by Lester B. Brown, PhD (Vol. 6, No. 2, 1997). *"A must read for educators, social workers, and other providers of social and mental health services." (Wynne DuBray, Professor, Division of Social Work, California State University)*

Social Services for Senior Gay Men and Lesbians, edited by Jean K. Quam, PhD, MSW (Vol. 6, No. 1, 1997). *"Provides a valuable overview of social service issues and practice with elder gay men and lesbians." (Outword)*

Men of Color: A Context for Service to Homosexually Active Men, edited by John F. Longres, PhD (Vol. 5, No. 2/3, 1996). *"An excellent book for the 'helping professions.' " (Feminist Bookstore News)*

Health Care for Lesbians and Gay Men: Confronting Homophobia and Heterosexism, edited by K. Jean Peterson, DSW (Vol. 5, No. 1, 1996). *"Essential reading for those concerned with the quality of health care services." (Etcetera)*

Sexual Identity on the Job: Issues and Services, edited by Alan L. Ellis, PhD, and Ellen D. B. Riggle, PhD (Vol. 4, No. 4, 1996). *"Reveals a critical need for additional research to address the many questions left unanswered or answered unsatisfactorily by existing research." (Sex Roles: A Journal of Research) "A key resource for addressing sexual identity concerns and issues in your workplace." (Outlines)*

Human Services for Gay People: Clinical and Community Practice, edited by Michael Shernoff, MSW, ACSW (Vol. 4, No. 2, 1996). *"This very practical book on clinical and community practice issues belongs on the shelf of every social worker, counselor, or therapist working with lesbians and gay men." (Gary A. Lloyd, PhD, ACSW, BCD, Professor and Coordinator, Institute for Research and Training in HIV/AIDS Counseling, School of Social Work, Tulane University)*

Violence in Gay and Lesbian Domestic Partnerships, edited by Claire M. Renzetti, PhD, and Charles Harvey Miley, PhD (Vol. 4, No. 1, 1996). *"A comprehensive guidebook for service providers and community and church leaders." (Small Press Magazine)*

Gays and Lesbians in Asia and the Pacific: Social and Human Services, edited by Gerard Sullivan, PhD, and Laurence Wai-Teng Leong, PhD (Vol. 3, No. 3, 1995). *"Insights in this book can provide an understanding of these cultures and provide an opportunity to better understand your own." (The Lavendar Lamp)*

Lesbians of Color: Social and Human Services, edited by Hilda Hidalgo, PhD, ACSW (Vol. 3, No. 2, 1995). *"An illuminating and helpful guide for readers who wish to increase their understanding of and sensitivity toward lesbians of color and the challenges they face." (Black Caucus of the ALA Newsletter)*

Lesbian Social Services: Research Issues, edited by Carol T. Tully, PhD, MSW (Vol. 3, No. 1, 1995). *"Dr. Tully challenges us to reexamine theoretical conclusions that relate to lesbians. . . A must read." (The Lavendar Lamp)*

HIV Disease: Lesbians, Gays and the Social Services, edited by Gary A. Lloyd, PhD, ACSW, and Mary Ann Kuszelewicz, MSW, ACSW (Vol. 2, No. 3/4, 1995). *"A wonderful guide to working with people with AIDS. A terrific meld of political theory and hands-on advice, it is essential, inspiring reading for anyone fighting the pandemic or assisting those living with it." (Small Press)*

Addiction and Recovery in Gay and Lesbian Persons, edited by Robert J. Kus, PhD, RN (Vol. 2, No. 1, 1995). *"Readers are well-guided through the multifaceted, sometimes confusing, and frequently challenging world of the gay or lesbian drug user." (Drug and Alcohol Review)*

Helping Gay and Lesbian Youth: New Policies, New Programs, New Practice, edited by Teresa DeCrescenzo, MSW, LCSW (Vol. 1, No. 3/4, 1994). *"Insightful and up-to-date, this handbook covers several topics relating to gay and lesbian adolescents . . . It is must reading for social workers, educators, guidance counselors, and policymakers." (Journal of Social Work Education)*

Social Services for Gay and Lesbian Couples, edited by Lawrence A. Kurdek, PhD (Vol. 1, No. 2, 1994). *"Many of the unique issues confronted by gay and lesbian couples are addressed here." (Ambush Magazine)*

Social Services with Transgendered Youth

Gerald P. Mallon, DSW
Editor

Social Services with Transgendered Youth has been co-published simultaneously as *Journal of Gay & Lesbian Social Services*, Volume 10, Numbers 3/4 1999.

Harrington Park Press
an Imprint of
The Haworth Press, Inc.
New York • London • Oxford

Published by

Harrington Park Press, 10 Alice Street, Binghamton, NY 13904-1580

Harrington Park Press is an imprint of The Haworth Press, Inc., 10 Alice Street, Binghamton, NY 13904-1580 USA.

Social Services with Transgendered Youth has been co-published simultaneously as *Journal of Gay & Lesbian Social Services,* Volume 10, Numbers 3/4 1999.

The development, preparation, and publication of this work has been undertaken with great care. However, the publisher, employees, editors, and agents of The Haworth Press and all imprints of The Haworth Press, Inc., including The Haworth Medical Press® and Pharmaceutical Products Press®, are not responsible for any errors contained herein or for consequences that may ensue from use of materials or information contained in this work. Opinions expressed by the author(s) are not necessarily those of The Haworth Press, Inc.

Library of Congress Cataloging-in-Publication Data

Social services with transgendered youth / Gerald P. Mallon, editor.
     p. cm.
     "Co-published simultaneously as Journal of Gay & Lesbian Social Services, Volume 10, Numbers 3/4 1999."
     Includes bibliographical references and index.
     ISBN 1-56023-135-1 (alk. paper)–ISBN 1-56023-136-X (alk. paper)
     1. Transsexuals–Psychology. 2. Transsexuals–Mental health services. 3. Social work with youth. I. Mallon, Gerald P.
HQ77.9.S63 2000
362.7'083–dc21   99-058923

INDEXING & ABSTRACTING

Contributions to this publication are selectively indexed or abstracted in print, electronic, online, or CD-ROM version(s) of the reference tools and information services listed below. This list is current as of the copyright date of this publication. See the end of this section for additional notes.

- *AIDS Newsletter c/o CAB International/CAB ACCESS*
- *BUBL Information Service, an Internet-based Information Service for the UK higher education community <URL: http://bubl.ac.uk/>*
- *Cambridge Scientific Abstracts*
- *caredata CD: the social and community care database*
- *CNPIEC Reference Guide: Chinese National Directory of Foreign Periodicals*
- *Contemporary Women's Issues*
- *Criminal Justice Abstracts*
- *Digest of Neurology and Psychiatry*
- *ERIC Clearinghouse on Urban Education (ERIC/CUE)*
- *Family Studies Database (online and CD/ROM)*
- *Family Violence & Sexual Assault Bulletin*
- *Gay & Lesbian Abstracts*
- *GenderWatch*
- *HOMODOK/"Relevant" Bibliographic Database*
- *IBZ International Bibliography of Periodical Literature*
- *Index to Periodical Articles Related to Law*
- *Mental Health Abstracts (online through DIALOG)*
- *Referativnyi Zhurnal (Abstracts Journal of the All-Russian Institute of Scientific and Technical Information)*
- *Social Services Abstracts*
- *Social Work Abstracts*
- *Sociological Abstracts (SA)*

(continued)

- *Studies on Women Abstracts*
- *Violence and Abuse Abstracts: A Review of Current Literature on Interpersonal Violence (VAA)*

Special Bibliographic Notes related to special journal issues (separates) and indexing/abstracting:

- indexing/abstracting services in this list will also cover material in any "separate" that is co-published simultaneously with Haworth's special thematic journal issue or DocuSerial. Indexing/abstracting usually covers material at the article/chapter level.
- monographic co-editions are intended for either non-subscribers or libraries which intend to purchase a second copy for their circulating collections.
- monographic co-editions are reported to all jobbers/wholesalers/approval plans. The source journal is listed as the "series" to assist the prevention of duplicate purchasing in the same manner utilized for books-in-series.
- to facilitate user/access services all indexing/abstracting services are encouraged to utilize the co-indexing entry note indicated at the bottom of the first page of each article/chapter/contribution.
- this is intended to assist a library user of any reference tool (whether print, electronic, online, or CD-ROM) to locate the monographic version if the library has purchased this version but not a subscription to the source journal.
- individual articles/chapters in any Haworth publication are also available through the Haworth Document Delivery Service (HDDS).

Social Services
with Transgendered Youth

CONTENTS

DEDICATION

For Joyce Hunter

ABOUT THE EDITOR

Gerald P. Mallon, DSW, is Assistant Professor at the City University of New York at Hunter College School of Social Work. Dr. Mallon's research interests focus on the experience of gay, lesbian, bisexual and transgendered children, youth, and families within the context of child welfare service delivery. He is also the author of several books, including: *We Don't Exactly Get the Welcome Wagon: The Experience of Gay and Lesbian Adolescents in Child Welfare Systems* (Columbia University Press, 1998); *Foundations of Social Work Practice with Lesbians and Gay Persons* (The Haworth Press, Inc., 1998); *Let's Get This Straight: A Gay and Lesbian Affirming Approach to Child Welfare* (Columbia University Press, 2000) and *Working with Gay, Lesbian, Bisexual, Transgendered and Questioning Youth: A Practical Guide for Youth Workers* (Child Welfare League of America, in press).

FOREWORD

The articles in this groundbreaking collection provide an urgently needed resource for social workers, therapists, health care providers, attorneys, teachers, and myriad others who work with transgendered children and youth.

For a long time, clinical and academic scholarship on transgendered people has concentrated almost exclusively on sex reassignment for transsexual adults. When children and adolescents have been mentioned at all, the focus has been on "treating" gender variance as a presumptively pathological condition rather than on developing an objective body of information or promoting genuine understanding or acceptance of transgendered youth.

Sadly, the leading academics in this area have been preoccupied with justifying therapeutic efforts to "modify the child's cross-gender behavior to standard boy and girl behavior" (Green, 1995; Minter, 1999). Less judgmental approaches have been almost completely unexplored. As a result, social workers and other front-line social service professionals have been left to resolve the dilemma of how to provide effective and competent services to transgendered youth on their own, with little or no useful guidance from the professional literature.

Shannon Minter, Esq. is a staff attorney at the National Center for Lesbian Rights in San Francisco, California since 1993. In addition to directing NCLR's pioneering Immigration Project and Youth Project, Minter is a volunteer attorney with the San Francisco Bar Association HIV and Immigration Project and a founding member of the San Francisco/Bay Area Lesbian and Gay Immigration and Asylum Rights Task Force. He can be reached via e-mail at Minter@nclrights.org

[Haworth co-indexing entry note]: "Foreword." Minter, Shannon. Co-published simultaneously in *Journal of Gay & Lesbian Social Services* (Harrington Park Press, an imprint of The Haworth Press, Inc.) Vol. 10, No. 3/4, 1999, pp. xix-xxi; and: *Social Services with Transgendered Youth* (ed: Gerald P. Mallon) Harrington Park Press, an imprint of The Haworth Press, Inc., 1999, pp. xiii-xv. Single or multiple copies of this article are available for a fee from The Haworth Document Delivery Service [1-800-342-9678, 9:00 a.m. - 5:00 p.m. (EST). E-mail address: getinfo@haworthpressinc.com].

Social Services with Transgendered Youth is a report from those frontlines. For the first time, practitioners who have worked with a broad range of transgendered children and youth in a wide variety of settings have been given an opportunity to examine, reflect on, and share the fruits of that experience with others. Not surprisingly, the conclusions and recommendations that have emerged from that work differ from past perspectives in a number of important ways. First, the authors writing here have rejected efforts to alter or influence a young person's gender identity or sexual orientation as contrary to the core ethical mandates of neutrality, objectivity, and respect for the client's autonomy. Rather than purporting to prevent "later homosexuality or transsexuality" (Green, 1995), as much of the clinical literature has tended to do, these practitioners have focused on the far more ethical and achievable goals of helping clients to develop the personal and social resources to make informed choices and to discover and define their own identities.

Second, these authors have refused to accept the preconception of pathology at face value. By listening to transgendered youth and acknowledging the realities and complexities of their lives, they have identified a number of external stressors–from isolation and parental rejection to violence in communities and schools–that account for many of the social and emotional problems that clinicians have erroneously viewed as evidence of inherent psychopathology. As a result of that fundamental shift in perspective, these practitioners have developed interventions that are effective and empowering because they are grounded in a realistic understanding of the severe prejudice and hostility that most young transgendered people face, simply for being who they are.

Finally, these authors also depart from most existing scholarship in their willingness to grapple with the diversity of transgendered identities. Beyond simply paying lip service to the fact that transgendered youth are a part of every ethnicity and class, these essays not only include the experiences of young people from many different groups, but they also acknowledge that different cultures define "standard boy and girl behavior" (and thus what it means to be "transgendered") in different ways. Rather than attempting to deny that multiplicity, these authors resist the temptation to force young people into predetermined categories or to judge them by the practitioner's own cultural norms.

In sum, the articles in this collection provide a wealth of new information and new perspectives on transgendered children and youth. They will enable social service professionals and other youth advocates to move beyond outmoded approaches that have not been effective and that have sometimes caused great harm. Although future scholarship may well elaborate on the insights in this volume, there is no doubt that it has set a new standard of professional competence and care that will benefit transgendered young people and their families for years to come.

Shannon Minter, Esq.
National Center for Lesbian Rights
San Francisco, CA

REFERENCES

Green, R. (1995). Gender identity disorder in children. In G.O. Gabbard (Ed.), *Treatments of psychiatric disorders* (p. 2007). Washington, DC: American Psychiatric Press.

Minter, S. (1999). Diagnosis and treatment of gender identity disorder in children. In M. Rottnek (Ed.), *Sissies & tomboys: Gender nonconformity & homosexual childhood* (pp. 9-33). New York: New York University Press.

Preface:
An Ecological Perspective
of Social Work Practice
with Transgendered Persons

Part of the way in which our society maintains stereotypes and negative attitudes about transgendered persons is by refusing to consider them as a legitimate topic for discussion in our homes or educational institutions. Such silence allows stereotypes to be maintained because positive images that reflect the reality of transgendered persons have been extremely limited in the media and in the professional literature which guides our practice. Because many transgendered youth cannot comfortably or safely disclose their orientation in such an atmosphere, students and practitioners are therefore not exposed to the realities or the diversities of this population. Undoubtedly, there is a pressing need to provide accurate, relevant, and affirming information on and about transgendered youth.

Although content on social work practice with transgendered youth should be integrated into every area of the social work curriculum, it is in the foundations curriculum of social work practice, which is an introduction to social work practice for graduate students, where this material should be first introduced. In its standards for accreditation, The Council on Social Work Education (CSWE) makes it clear that "foundation curriculum must include content on social work values and ethics, diversity, social and economic justice, populations-at-risk, human behavior and the social environment, social welfare policy and services, social work prac-

[Haworth co-indexing entry note]: "Preface: An Ecological Perspective of Social Work Practice with Transgendered Persons." Mallon, Gerald P. Co-published simultaneously in *Journal of Gay & Lesbian Social Services* (Harrington Park Press, an imprint of The Haworth Press, Inc.) Vol. 10, No. 3/4, 1999, pp. xxiii-xxvii; and: *Social Services with Transgendered Youth* (ed: Gerald P. Mallon) Harrington Park Press, an imprint of The Haworth Press, Inc., 1999, pp. xvii-xxi. Single or multiple copies of this article are available for a fee from The Haworth Document Delivery Service [1-800-342-9678, 9:00 a.m. - 5:00 p.m. (EST). E-mail address: getinfo@haworthpressinc.com].

xvii

tice, research, and field practicum" (CSWE, 1992, p. 139). As part of this mandate, the Council's standard on "Populations-at-Risk" states: "Programs of social work education must present theoretical and practice content about patterns, dynamics, and consequences of discrimination, economic deprivation, and oppression. The curriculum must provide content about people of color, women, and gay and lesbian persons. Such content must emphasize the impact of discrimination, economic deprivation, and oppression upon these groups" (CSWE, 1992, p. 140).

Despite a baccalaureate liberal arts education, most of which is presumably devoid of any mention of transgendered youth, it is unlikely that graduate students entering the profession of social work will have foundation knowledge about transgendered youth. Despite mandates, they might not even receive much content about gay and lesbian persons in social work education, as most social work educators have been relatively unwilling or unresponsive in their approaches to integrating curriculum content on this population in any meaningful way. Despite its reputation as champions of the subjugated (Berger, 1977), social work has lagged behind psychiatry, psychology, and counseling in recognizing the legitimacy of transgendered youth, as evidenced by the actions of respective professional organizations, and the amount of attention which each discipline has given to the topic of transgendered youth in its literature.

This is the first collection of essays about transgendered persons which has embraced a social work professional's perspective. We see this collection as a Primer about Transgendered youth. The authors of these papers offer current knowledge about social work practice with transgendered youth. Although we are certain that this book will be useful to students and practitioners of social work, we hope that this book will be replaced by one that provides even greater knowledge within the next five years.

Within the context of a foundation base of knowledge for social work practice, begun in an earlier text (Mallon, 1998) which focused on gay and lesbian persons, this text sets forth the groundwork for social work practice with transgendered youth across system levels–individuals, groups, and families. Using an ecological perspective (Germain, 1973, 1978, 1981, 1991; German & Gitterman, 1980), the various authors of the papers collected herein, examine practice issues with transgendered youth from a holistic viewpoint where individuals and environments are understood as a unit, in the context of their relationship to one another (Germain, 1991, p. 16). Because strict boundaries regulate gender in our Western society, there are no acceptable ways to achieve full status as a person who identifies as transgendered when one is forced to be defined by traditional theories and environmental expectations.

Consequently, the contributors of these papers examine the primary reciprocal exchanges and transactions that transgendered youth face as they confront the unique person:environmental tasks involved in being a person in a society that assumes all of its members are gender defined at birth. As this text aims toward helping social work students and practitioners to increase their understanding of transgendered youth by introducing them to a foundation level of knowledge, the focus of this book is limited to discussions regarding social work practice, within the context of practice with individuals, groups, couples, and families.

The interventions and strategies discussed within the various client system levels are positively aimed at improving one's social functioning, identifying client strengths, and are focused on an affirming stance which emphasizes resilience and health as opposed to an approach which is based on deficit and pathology. Helping transgendered youth to move toward a goodness of fit within an oftentimes hostile environment is the foundation on which these authors have based their work.

Given social work's purpose, it is clear that social workers need to understand how to practice with diverse populations, including transgendered persons. Fundamental to this process is the requirement that social work practitioners develop strong assessment skills. Adequate assessment in social work, noted Meyer (1993, p. 12) requires practitioners "to think big, to see the full transactional process all at once." Social workers preparing to practice with transgendered youth, however, must do more than just think big, they must also think broadly in their conceptualization of gender identity and think beyond the presumed assumption that all people are clearly male or female in their gender identification. Thinking and acting beyond one's personal, religious, or cultural biases are additional ingredients that practitioners who work with clients that identify as transgendered must learn to add to their repertoire of skills.

This text emerged from my discussions at professional conferences, twenty-four years of practice experiences, for the last twelve primarily with gay, lesbian, bisexual, and transgendered adolescents in out-of-home child welfare settings, and dialogues in academic settings with colleagues and students about the state of the art of transgendered practice issues. We agreed that transgendered youth were frequently overlooked by both practitioners and educators, and also felt strongly that this was an area which was ripe for exploration.

Divided into eight papers, eight scholars and practitioners in the area of social work practice with gay and lesbian persons have provided fundamental concepts and groundwork for others who wish to prepare for social work practice with transgendered youth.

Although this book focuses exclusively on practice with transgendered youth, the first paper provides an overview of the conceptual knowledge base of practice with transgendered persons across the developmental spectrum. It examines a knowledge base of practice in several major areas: practice wisdom, personal experiences, a historical context, knowledge of the literature, research, information derived from the case, and analysis of theory and concepts. The second essay provides a skillful analysis of the values and ethics which guide social work professionals in their practice with transgendered youth. The next two essays examine transgendered identity in childhood, and practice approaches for working with this group.

The next two papers explore the various systemic levels of practice with transgendered male to female youth and female to male youth. Klein's essay examines practice with transgendered youth who prostitute within the group context. The essay by Cooper surveys practice issues that affect transgendered youth within families. A final essay proposes organizational strategies to enhance the provision of services to transgendered youth.

Each of the papers has an excellent and comprehensive reference list that should help the novice and the experienced practitioner continue in their quest toward practicing competently with transgendered clients in a variety of systems. A glossary of words and phrases commonly used by transgendered persons is provided to act as a guide for terms used throughout the text. Practice issues are summarized in the Guide to Staff Self-Awareness.

Gerald P. Mallon, DSW

REFERENCES

Berger, R.M. (1977) An advocate model for intervention with homosexuals. *Social Work, 22* (4), 280-283.

Council on Social Work Education. (1992). *Curriculum policy statement for master's degree programs in social work education.* Alexandria, VA: Council on Social Work Education.

Germain, C. B. (1973). The ecological perspective in casework practice. *Social Casework: The Journal of Contemporary Social Work, 54*, 323-330.

Germain, C. B. (1978). General-systems theory and ego psychology: An ecological perspective. *Social Service Review*, 535-550.

Germain, C. B. (1981). The ecological approach to people-environment transactions. *Social Casework: The Journal of Contemporary Social Work, 62*, 323-331.

Germain, C. B. (1991). *Human behavior and the social environment*. New York: Columbia University Press.

Germain, C. B., & Gitterman, A. (1980). *The life model of social work practice*. New York: Columbia University Press.

Germain, C. B., & Gitterman, A. (1996). *The life model of social work practice* (2nd ed.). New York: Columbia University Press.

Mallon, G. (1998). *Foundations of social work practice with gay and lesbian persons*. Binghamton, NY: Haworth.

Meyer, C. (1993). *Assessment in social work practice*. New York: Columbia University Press.

Acknowledgments

The idea for writing this Special Issue came from discussions I had with Ray Berger who is Volunteer Honorary Editor of *Journal of Gay & Lesbian Social Services*. His tireless quest to help practitioners and scholars to think about and write about gay, lesbian, bisexual, and transgendered persons has allowed me to write papers and edit special issue journals that speak to the needs of persons whose voices have been marginalized. Ray's commitment to this task has made him a genuine role model for me, and he makes writing for the *Journal* an indisputable pleasure.

My immediate thanks is due next to those practitioners and scholars who agreed to author the papers collected in this volume. In asking each of these professionals to participate in this project it was important for me that they be trained social work practitioners and educators. I am proud that many of the authors have been my former students at Hunter College School of Social Work or at Columbia University School of Social Work. They had in my classes written so passionately about transgendered persons, that when I asked them to submit papers for this volume, their enthusiasm and their eagerness for doing so made this a very stimulating project for me to be involved in.

Although I am grateful to all of those authors who contributed, I must pay special homage to one of the authors–Wendell Glenn from the Gay and Lesbian Social Services (GLASS) in Los Angeles. Wendell has been my mentor and my very best teacher about the lives of transgendered youth. One afternoon in a Taco Restaurant on Santa Monica Boulevard and Robertson, in West Hollywood, he changed my life. Wendell's courage and honesty in sharing his story with me allowed me, for the first time, to really understand what it means for some people to be transgendered. Wendell's deep commitment to transgendered youth and his ability to convey their experiences to me helped to free me from my own ignorance and judgment. I will always be indebted to him for sharing this knowledge with me and for contributing to opening my mind and my heart to being a better practitioner.

My thanks is also extended to my partner, Mike Rendino, who has always supplied me with a relationship and home environment that has sustained me and given me a life outside of my work. His unending patience when I take "just a few minutes" to clean up a paper or a few hours to "do some real writing" is laudable. My family, which also includes Ian, Travis, and Leslie, who give me so much enjoyment, is what makes all of this work worthwhile. I am grateful beyond words to them.

Finally, I would like to thank my colleague and good friend, Joyce Hunter. Twenty years ago, when I was deep in the closet, I saw Joyce on a news program, speaking out and advocating for gay and lesbian youth. I thought then, as I still think now–"What a brave woman!" Joyce has been my inspiration in doing the work that I do. She has always been there for me whenever I have needed her and through it all, Joyce has been my good friend, which for me is the most important role she could have in my life. For this reason and for others which are rooted in deep feelings and not possible to express in words, this book is dedicated to her.

Gerald P. Mallon, DSW

Knowledge for Practice
with Transgendered Persons

Gerald P. Mallon

SUMMARY. Most social work practitioners have had very limited knowledge about or information to inform their practice with transgendered persons, but cultivating a knowledge base of practice to prepare students to work more competently and effectively with transgendered persons is an essential element of good practice and needs to be integrated into a foundation level social work curriculum in meaningful and conscientious ways. The following paper explores the theme of knowledge for practice with transgendered persons by examining seven areas from where social work practice is derived. *[Article copies available for a fee from The Haworth Document Delivery Service: 1-800-342-9678. E-mail address: getinfo@haworthpressinc.com <Website: http://www.haworthpressinc.com>]*

KEYWORDS. Transgendered youth, social work practice, narratives, social work education curriculum

INTRODUCTION

"You have it all wrong, Gary, I am not gay, I am transgendered. I may have the biological body of a male, but inside, I am a woman. I am heterosexual, and I am a female." So said my 17 year old client to me one day, and I thought after he told me this, "You are daft. If you

Gerald P. Mallon, DSW, is Assistant Professor, Hunter College School of Social Work, New York City, NY.

[Haworth co-indexing entry note]: "Knowledge for Practice with Transgendered Persons." Mallon, Gerald P. Co-published simultaneously in *Journal of Gay & Lesbian Social Services* (Harrington Park Press, an imprint of The Haworth Press, Inc.) Vol. 10, No. 3/4, 1999, pp. 1-18; and: *Social Services with Transgendered Youth* (ed: Gerald P. Mallon) Harrington Park Press, an imprint of The Haworth Press, Inc., 1999, pp. 1-18. Single or multiple copies of this article are available for a fee from The Haworth Document Delivery Service [1-800-342-9678, 9:00 a.m. - 5:00 p.m. (EST). E-mail address: getinfo@haworthpressinc.com].

have a penis, then you are a male and no matter what you'd like to be, or see yourself as, you are a male." How ignorant I was, and how uninformed I was about transgendered persons. I didn't realize as activist Riki Anne Wilchins (Goldberg, 1999, p. B2) said, "It's not about what's between my legs."

Just as those who did not understand their circumstances or their nature had called gay, lesbian, and bisexual persons crazy, transgendered persons have been even more misunderstood. If social work practitioners are ill-prepared to deal with gay and lesbian persons (and in most cases they are) then certainly they are unprepared to respond to the needs of transgendered persons. As a practitioner with almost twenty years of experience, many of them with gay, lesbian, bisexual, and questioning clients, I felt very inadequate myself in attempting to deal with clients who identified as transgendered. Apart from its significance as a practice dilemma, this case also illustrates an important truth about transgendered persons in contemporary society: That most people, even experienced practitioners, have little or no accurate knowledge about the lives of transgendered persons.

AN ECOLOGICAL APPROACH

The person:environment perspective, loosely utilized throughout this text as a framework for practice, has been a central influence on the profession's theoretical base and has usefulness and relevance as an approach to social work practice with transgendered persons. Gitterman and Germain (1996, p. 19) underscore the point that disempowerment, which threatens the health, social well-being, and life of those who are oppressed, imposes enormous adaptive tasks on transgendered persons. An understanding of the destructive relationships which exist between transgendered persons and an environment that is focused on "either\or" male or female gender constructions is integral to the process of developing practice knowledge about working with trangendered persons as clients. The purpose of this paper, then, is to define, identify, and describe the knowledge base of practice with transgendered persons and to review social work's response to the needs of this population.

What the social worker is supposed to do should dictate the boundaries of the profession's knowledge base, noted Meyer (1982). If social workers are supposed to be able to work with transgendered persons, then a knowledge-base for practice with them must be within those boundaries. An organized knowledge base is crucial to any profession. Anyone, notes Mattaini (1995, p. 6), "can act." The professional, however, is expected to act deliberately, taking the steps that are most likely to be helpful, least intrusive, and consistent with the person's welfare. Making a conscious determination about those choices requires an extensive knowledge base.

SOURCES OF KNOWLEDGE

In a chapter in an earlier book which focuses on the acquisition of knowledge for foundation practice, Mallon (1998) identifies several key sources of knowledge, which in a modified version herein, provide a framework for this paper's discussion on knowledge for practice with transgendered persons. Sources identified by Mallon include: (1) practice wisdom derived from narrative experiences of the profession and professional colleagues, (2) the personal experiences of the practitioner, (3) a knowledge of the professional literature, (4) a knowledge of history and current events, (5) research issues which inform practice, (6) theoretical and conceptual analyses, and (7) information which is provided by the case itself. All of these, understood within an ecological framework of person:environment, with a consciousness of the reality of oppression in the lives of transgendered persons, is called upon to inform social work practice with transgendered persons and each contributes to the development of the knowledge base of practice with this population.

PRACTICE WISDOM

Practice wisdom can be viewed as that which is derived from the narrative experiences of the profession, from both professional colleagues and from clients. Although narrative experiences may have drawbacks, in that one person's experience is not generalizable to the experiences of many, listening to the life stories of clients and permitting them to tell their story in their own words is central to the experience of social work practice (Mason-Schrock, 1996).

Interest in narrative theory has grown in recent years and the use of life stories in practice has, in some organizations, replaced elaborate, formalized intake histories. Life stories, which tend to be rich in detail, are usually obtained early in the work with a client and can be a useful means toward not only gathering important data to enhance one's knowledge-base, but useful in establishing a rapport and a trusting relationship with a transgendered client. As the client tells and the worker listens empathetically, in the telling and the listening, the story gains personal and cultural meanings. This process, particularly with transgendered persons who have been oppressed, marginalized, and silenced, can also be a healing process. It is, as Germain and Gitterman (1996, p. 145) put it, "our human way of finding meaning in life events, of explaining our life experience to ourselves and others, so that we can move on."

Social work practitioners, however, should be cautious about utilizing practice wisdom, especially when most social workers have probably had very limited experience with transgendered persons. That being said, listening to life stories can inform practice in a meaningful way. If one listens to, really listens to the narratives, with the third ear, and then connects the themes with past practice-based data obtained from previous practice, it can help to make sense of the situation and to guide one's practice (Parlee, 1996).

In addition to listening to the life stories of clients, and the practice experiences of practitioners, social workers practicing with transgendered persons can rely on rules which have been handed down by experienced practitioners that appear to work. Although practice with transgendered persons is a very new area of practice, heuristic practice which can be described as principles to guide patterns of professional behavior, and that which has shaped and refined practice may also serve as models for other workers. The acquisition of group-specific language to guide practice, and a knowledge of the myths and stereotypes about transgendered persons can be extremely useful forms of heuristic practice. A glossary of terms and several of the most common myths as well as guidelines to competent practice with transgendered persons can be found in the Glossary in this text. Such fragments of practice wisdom can be valuable as a guide for practitioners interested in enhancing their practice knowledge base in working with transgendered persons.

PERSONAL EXPERIENCE

The personal experience of practitioners is the second powerful force which guides knowledge development. Although social workers are guided not only by their own personal experiences, but by a Professional Code of Ethics, most social workers base some of their knowledge about clients by integrating and synthesizing events gathered from their own life experiences. Within the guidelines provided by the profession's Code of Ethics, basic interpersonal and problem-solving skills that social workers have developed throughout their lives are an important means toward informing one's practice (Moore, 1999).

It is a myth that most people do not know anyone who is transgendered, but unquestionably, social workers who have a close friend or a family member who is openly dealing with gender issues, may have additional personal experiences that can assist them in guiding their practice with this population. Additionally, social workers who are themselves transgendered will unquestionably have additional insights into transgendered clients. However, being transgendered alone does not provide a practitioner with a complete and full knowledge for practice with transgendered clients. Individuals who are transgendered-identified themselves may be at various stages of their own sexual identity development and their knowledge may be, at best, incomplete. Professional practice requires that practitioners conduct themselves in ways that are consistent with professional values and ethics.

Issues of self-disclosure become significant when a social worker has had personal experiences or shares something in common with a client, in this case a transgendered identity. A transgendered practitioner may find it helpful to disclose his or her orientation with a client who is struggling with whether or not to come out, but in other cases, the worker's disclosure could inhibit the client from sharing genuine feelings (Gartrell, 1994). Although self-disclosure can be useful in many cases, and while practitioners are using self-disclosure more than they did in the past, social workers need, at a minimum, close supervision and consultation to process these issues. Although personal experiences are key in knowledge development, social workers must always be in touch with their own feelings (Greene, 1994) and must remember that self-disclosure always has to do with the well-being of the client, not the practitioner.

HISTORY AND CURRENT EVENTS

Because practice is embedded in the broader social context of life, knowledge of the social policies and shifting social forces is important for knowledge development and working with transgendered persons. Because historical events are most often documented in the news media, newspapers, and other information from multiple media sources can be important sources of information (Park, 1998). News stories and talk shows in the mass media are often less than objective and in many cases replete with inaccuracies; however, for many, these are the only sources of knowledge about gay men and lesbians and an important basis to work from, even in a professional context.

The media, especially the talk show circuit–Jerry Springer, Ricki Lake, Sally Jesse Raphael, Jenny Jones, and others–have all made a great deal of money by sensationalizing the stories of individuals who are somewhere on the transgendered spectrum. Some social workers may feel that these shows provide a baseline of information about transgendered persons, but for the most part, they only impart misinformation and perpetuate myths.

The Internet or the World Wide Web has provided another very important source of information that individuals can obtain within the confines of their own homes. The Information Superhighway has not only grown exponentially during the past several years, but has also provided a plethora of new information about a wide variety of topics pertaining to transgendered persons. Although there are also inaccuracies on the Internet, one huge benefit for those seeking access to knowledge about transgendered persons is that the Web has a reach that exceeds geography. Consequently, persons in remote rural areas, as well as those in more urban centers have equal ability to gather information about and communicate with transgendered persons around the world, whereas in the past such data were only to be found in urban environs. Although one must have access to a computer to make such connections, libraries and schools in many communities can provide individuals with such access.

A recent scan of relevant Web Sites includes: The Transgender Forum (www.tgforum.com), Transsexual Menace (www.apocalypse.org/pub/tsmenace), Transworld (www.qworld.org/friends/transworld), and Transgender Community Forum (members.aol.com/onqgwen/index/html). All maintain careful watch on a wide array of issues that affect transgendered persons. These are but a few Web sites of the literally thousands that exist on the topic of transgendered persons. The reader may find others through links with any of the Web sites mentioned above, or may find additional sites by using one of the numerous Search Engines (Yahoo, Webcrawler, Lycos, Hotbot, Excite, Metacrawler, and others) and by keying code words and phrases such as: transgender, FTM, MTF, transgendered, transsexual, gender identity, and gender diversity.

Social work's history with transgendered persons can best be described as an invisible relationship. Although the Delegate Assembly of the National Association of Social Workers (Moore, 1999) has proposed to adopt a policy statement on Transgender Issues/Gender Identity Issues which emphasized its ban on discrimination based on gender identity issues, social work has generally lagged behind other helping professionals in putting resources behind its commitment.

Although the Council on Social Work Education (1992) revised its Accreditation Standards to require schools of Social Work to include foundation content related to lesbian and gay service needs and practice into the core course curriculum (see Humphreys, 1983; Newman, 1989), there has been no such movement toward the integration of transgender or gender identity issues into the curriculum. Such reticence signals a reluctance on the part of the professional to allow transgendered persons full and equal access to inclusion in the curriculum.

Despite inclusive policies and accreditation mandates that call for nondiscriminatory professional practice, an inherent difficulty in separating personal attitudes from professional prerogatives with respect to transgendered identity issues appears to have made service provision to this population a complex process. While homosexuality has historically been and continues to be a taboo subject for discussion even within most professional climates (Gochros, 1985, 1995; Mallon, 1992a), transgender identity seems to be even more taboo.

THE PROFESSIONAL LITERATURE

Although many authors of articles that focus on gay, lesbian, and bisexual clients add the term "transgender" to these titles, few genuinely focus on the unique needs of this population. Indeed, a very limited assemblage of professional literature has been published in the professional social work literature that specifically focuses the social service needs of transgendered persons. A Socio-Lit, Psych-Lit and Social Work Abstracts computer search using the words "transgender youth" yielded no articles. Those articles which do exist of the broader transgender population center almost exclusively on transsexuals or on sexual re-assignment surgery (Braunthal, 1981; Chong, 1990; Oles, 1977; Williams, 1997). With the publication of this collection of essays, *Journal of Gay & Lesbian Social Services (JGLSS)* is the first social work journal to initiate a dialogue about the experiences of transgendered youth. Brown (1997) produced an earlier edition of *JGLSS*, which explored the phenomenon of two-spirited transgendered persons; Jackson and Sullivan (1999) edited a Special Issue of *JGLSS* that investigated transgendered experiences from a Thai viewpoint.

Surprisingly, *Journal of Homosexuality*, the most senior of the gay and lesbian affirming journals, has published only one article in the past five years that focuses on transgendered persons (Lombardi, 1999). Mainstream social work publications (*Social Work, Social Services Review* and *Families in Society*) have also made modest progress in publishing articles in this area.

If one were to look exclusively within the social work professional literature to develop a knowledge-base of practice, one would find a very circumscribed discussion of transgendered practice issues in the mainstream social work literature. Although it appears that the major social work journals have been slow to respond to and to publish articles which address the wide and diverse needs of transgendered persons, in fairness, it is not possible to know how many articles have been submitted and rejected, or how many in total have been submitted on this population. Two articles, both over twenty years old, and now out of date in their practice approaches to working with transgendered persons, were all that were available several years ago when I struggled to put together a class on the transgendered experience (Levine, 1978; Wicks, 1977). I list them here simply because the authors of these papers should be acknowledged for the risks they took in publishing this material at the time they did.

For a fuller understanding of practice with transgendered persons, particularly with transgendered youth, practitioners would be wise to look outside of social work for guidance. For professionals who work with individuals with gender identity issues, Israel and Tarver's (1997) excellent sourcebook provides practitioners with a wide breadth of information and resources about transgendered persons. Its focus on recommended guidelines, practical information and personal narratives address issues of cultural diversity, sexual orientation, and transsexual life that have been previously ignored in the clinical literature.

Bornstein's (1994, 1998) books provide practitioners with insight into the transworld, from a transgendered person's perspective. Feinberg's (1993) deservedly honored classic–*Stone Butch Blues*, and her more scholarly work, *Transgender Warriors: Making History from Joan of Arc to Dennis Rodman* provide social work practitioners with valuable knowledge-building insights.

Transgendered activists Daphne Scholinski (1997) and Phyllis Burke (1997), from personal experiences, have documented the brutal adversion therapies to which gender identity disordered (GID) diagnoses, gender-variant youth have been subjected to coerce them into conformity. Riki Anne Wilchins (1997) raises many provocative questions about the oppressive nature of gender classification, and her final chapter documenting hate crimes against transsexuals' underscores the urgency with which Wilchins questions language and gender exclusion. Volcano and Halberstam (1999) introduce readers to the experiences and culture of the Drag Kings community.

Randi Ettner's (1996) book *Confessions of a Gender Defender*, provides first-hand insights into a psychologist's reflections on life among transgendered persons. Ettner's book helps clinicians examine their own gaps in training and helps to assess their own counter-transference issues surrounding treatment of transgendered persons. Ettner and Brown's (1999) latest work is a comprehensive guide to understanding and treating individuals with gender issues. The book provides an overview of the field, including the history, etiology, diagnosis, research, and treatment of gender variant persons.

Although this is a very medically-oriented text and relies heavily on viewing transgendered persons from a pathological perspective, Zucker and Bradley's (1995) volume provides an in-depth, authoritative overview on the diagnosis, assessment, etiology and treatment of gender identity disorder from a childhood and adolescent perspective.

RESEARCH

If the research on gay and lesbian persons is slim, the research on transgendered persons is almost non-existent. Again, the research that does exist focuses almost exclusively on sexual re-assignment surgery for transsexual persons. In cases where little quantitative empirical evidence is found, naturalistic research methods have increasingly been seen as particularly effective means of informing social work practice. These naturalistic means, particularly narrative approaches, may prove to be useful for social work practitioners.

THEORETICAL AND CONCEPTUAL ANALYSES

Theories to guide practice or theoretical constructs, which help one to better understand and practice with a client system also offer explanations to guide practice. Understanding the process of transgendered identity formation will undoubtedly enable the practitioner to carry out informed and sensitive intervention with clients and families struggling with issues of gender identity. However, practitioners must also be aware of the fact that it is not possible for them to utilize tradition developmental models taught in most human behavior and the social environment sequences (Erikson, 1950; Marcia, 1980; Offer, 1980; Offer, Ostrov, & Howard, 1981) which posit concepts of sex-role identifications which are concerned only with heterosexual development and presume heterosexual identity as an eventual outcome. Utilizing these traditional approaches, which view transgender identity from a developmentally pejorative perspective, does not assist or prepare the practitioner to work competently with transgendered persons.

Unlike their counterparts in the heterosexual majority, those individuals on the transgender spectrum experience a social condition which is attributable to their transgendered orientation–oppression, stigmatization, and marginalization. Oppression, notes Pharr (1988, p. 53), cannot be viewed in isolation because they are interconnected: sexism, racism, homophobia, classism, anti-Semitism, and ableism, and are linked by a common origin–economic power and control. Backed by institutional power, economic power, and both institutional and individual violence, this trinity of elements acts as the "standard of rightness and often righteousness wherein all others are judged in relation to it."

There are many ways that norms are enforced both by individuals and institutions. One way to view persons who fall outside the "norm" is to label such individuals as *"the other."* It is easy to discriminate against, view as deviant, marginal, or inferior, such groups that are not part of the mainstream. Those who are classified as such, become part of an invisible minority, a group whose achievements are kept hidden and unknown from those in the dominant culture. Stereotyping, blaming the victim, distortion of reality, can even lead the person to feeling as though they deserve the oppression which they experience. This process is called internalized transgenderphobia (Norton, 1997; Park, 1998). Other elements of oppression include: isolation, self-hatred, underachievement or over-achievement, substance abuse, problems with relationships and a variety of other mental health matters.

Violence, as suggested by Lombardi et al. (1998), Herek (1990) and Pharr (1988), is also seen as a theoretical construct in the lives of transgendered persons. The threat of violence toward transgendered persons, particularly transgendered youth who must attend community schools, is made all the more powerful by the fact that they do not have to do anything to receive the violence. It is their lives alone that precipitate such action. Therefore, transpersons always have a sense of safety which is fragile and tenuous and they may never feel completely secure. Social workers who are unfamiliar with transpersons may view such conditions as a pathology in need of treatment, but for the transgendered person such insecurity is an adaptive strategy for living within in a hostile environment (Germain & Gitterman, 1996).

SELF-AWARENESS

Many students entering the world of social work, think that they are open-minded and while many may have a genuine desire to help others, some have not delved inside of themselves to assess the role that power, privilege, and influence have played in their own lives.

As social work is a values-based profession (Mc Gowan, 1995), we are ethically obligated to address these issues and to work toward increasing the levels of competence and awareness within both students entering the professional and colleagues who continue to make contributions. Although the professional literature has begun to address these areas, as professionals we also must focus on the issue of self-awareness.

The consequence of not considering theoretical analyses and concepts which are transphobic is that many heterosexual social workers believe that if they avoid society's fear and loathing of transgendered persons then that is all that they will need to do to work effectively with trangendered clients. While most social workers have "politically correct" ideas about gay men and lesbians, many professionals have not always had the opportunity to deal with the deeper prejudices and heterosexual privileges that they possess. Since most professionals continue to have an inadequate knowledge base about the real lives of transgendered persons, this causes them, to be in many cases, more transignorant than trans-phobic.

Many transgendered persons believe that heterosexually-oriented social workers still harbor the heterocentric assumption that it is less than normal or less preferable to be transgendered. Some social workers, particularly those from a more psychoanalytically-oriented perspective, believe that somewhere in the transgendered person's system you can find the roots or the cause of transgendered identity, and that it secretly has something to do with family dysfunction or childhood sexual abuse.

The abolition of Gender Identity Disorder from the D.S.M. (American Psychiatric Association, 1994) is another important issue for social workers to consider. What most workers do not realize, according to Park (1998, p. 16), is that "GID, as defined in the D.S.M. IV, also represents an effort by the medico-psychiatric establishment to "cure" homosexuality, 25 years after the APA removed homosexuality from its catalogue of mental illnesses. Although GID is ostensibly only about gender identity and not sexual orientation, it is striking that the DSM-IV advises that psychiatrists note "specifiers" based on the individual's sexual orientation . . . if GID were exclusively concerned with gender identity, why would the APA feel compelled to advise clinicians to note orientation?" Although this has been a serious issue of contention, the good news is that the APA has appointed a working group on GID to re-examine the GID diagnosis in preparation for the revision that will produce the DSM-V.

These are complex issues which need to be addressed within the overall context of diversity and yet at the same time, from a specific transgendered perspective. Moral, religious, and cultural biases still run deep in many students preparing for practice and in professionals who currently practice. Although there are no simple solutions to helping individuals overcome their biases, beginning an honest dialogue and providing students with accurate and appropriate information about gay men and lesbians is an important place to start.

KNOWLEDGE DERIVED FROM THE INDIVIDUAL CASE

Information, which is provided by the case itself, is the final means toward the generation of knowledge about transgendered persons that will be discussed in this paper. The individual, couple, or family system and the environmental context within which they live provide a great deal of information that is specific to the case and which can guide practice. Listening to what clients, say, and observing what they do from initial engagement, through assessment, intervention and termination, can provide crucial information.

Although some transgendered persons present concerns that relate specifically to issues of gender orientation, many of which will be discussed in Pazos' and Glenn's essays in this collection, these individuals, "usually seek help for a range of issues that have little to do with their sexual orientation per se or are related to it in an indirect way." Like their heterosexual counterparts, transgendered persons seek help from social work practitioners to deal with a wide array of problems in living.

A critical aspect of intervening with a client who identifies as transgendered is for practitioners to have a firm understanding of the client's identity formation (see Burgess's essay in this collection).

The practitioner who is sensitive and affirming in his or her work with transgendered persons needs to have a complete understanding of the psychological, behavioral, affectional, attitudinal, and an internal sense of "goodness of fit" as the features of each of the stages of coming out and direct their interventions accordingly. A lack of familiarity with this process will cause the practitioner to misinterpret the client's reactions and miss opportunities to assist the client in moving forward in the process of developing a comfort with their own identity.

Practitioners need to be aware that certain conditions may be intensified, if not caused by oppression and stigmatization to which transgendered youth may have been exposed in their development and which they may continue to experience as adults. For example, although the coming out process has been conceptualized as a positive developmental step toward healthfulness, the societal or familial response to an individual's disclosure may be less than constructive.

Social work practitioners need to be sensitive to the particular needs and concerns of the transgendered person and must also appreciate that the client's membership in a stigmatized and oppressed group

(Goffman, 1963) has shaped his or her identity and may play a role in the presenting problem which they may or may not bring to their initial session. Whether or not the presenting problem is related to the client's sexual orientation, the practitioner who intervenes with the client must be well-acquainted with the issues and features of transgendered life, develop an expertise in working with the population and acquire a knowledge of the community resources which exist to help this client. It is also important to recognize that there is as much diversity in the transgendered community as in all other communities, and therefore, there is no one type of transgendered individual.

Although Western society has made some positive steps toward altering negative attitudes toward gay men and lesbians, practitioners must be aware of the presence of the phenomenon of transgenderphobia (Park, 1998) and a client's own internalized transgenderphobia. Workers must help clients refrain from reinforcing it through their own bias and stereotypes. Isolation is another problem that frequently arises as a result of the stigma associated with a transgendered identity. Practitioners need to be knowledgeable about resources which exist in the community and if necessary to support clients by going with them to visit these resources. The development of social support networks through involvement in such programs can be an important task for the client and practitioner to work on together.

Subsequent papers in this collection will focus on exploring social work practice with transgendered persons from the perspectives of several client systems: individuals, groups, and families.

CONCLUSIONS

The social work profession recognizes that a person's gender identity does not always conform to her or his gender at birth. Transgendered persons should be afforded the same respect and rights as those whose gender identity is the same as their biologically given gender. Discrimination, oppression, and prejudice directed against any group is damaging to the social, emotional, and economic well-being of the affected group, as well as to society as a whole. All social workers are ethically bound to fight to eliminate such discrimination inside and outside the profession, in both public and private sectors.

Adopting nonjudgmental attitudes toward gender identity enables social workers to provide maximum support and services to those who are part of the transgendered community. Social workers and the profession can support and empower transgendered persons through all phases of their coming out process. Utilizing ecological approaches that assist persons in developing adaptation to their environments, social workers should also be aware that they may need to assist in developing supportive practice environments for those struggling with gender identity, both among clients and colleagues.

Cultivating a knowledge base of practice to prepare students and practitioners to work more competently and effectively with transgendered persons, especially with transgendered youth, is an essential element of good practice and needs to be integrated into a foundation level curriculum in meaningful and conscientious ways. The Council on Social Work Education should require course content on transgender issues, offer research opportunities for investigating issues of relevance to this population, develop and provide training for instructors and students, and seek out field opportunities for students interested in working with transgendered persons.

On a societal level we must work to eliminate the psychological and physical harm directed at transgendered persons and to work toward portraying them accurately and compassionately. Programs that address the health and mental health needs of clients must work toward developing sensitive and respectful practice with transgendered persons and their families.

From a legal and political action perspective, social workers need to join together with other professional associations and progressive organizations to lobby on behalf of the civil rights of transgendered persons. An increase in funding for education, treatment services, and research on behalf of transgendered persons is essential. Finally, the repeal of laws that impede individuals from identifying with the gender of their choice and insuring that individuals will not suffer discrimination against them in inheritance, insurance, child custody, and property are both part of the proud tradition of social work's mission to fight for social justice for all people.

REFERENCES

American Psychiatric Association. (1994). *Diagnostic and Statistical Manual of Mental Disorders (4th edition)* (pp. 537-538). Washington, D.C.: Author.
Bornstein, K. (1994). *Gender outlaw: On men, women, and the rest of us.* New York: Routledge.

Bornstein, K. (1998). *My gender workbook.* New York: Routledge.

Braunthal, H. (1981). Working with transsexuals. *International Journal of Social Psychiatry, 27* (1), 3-11.

Brown, L.B. (1997). *Two-spirited people: American Indian lesbian women and gay men,* New York: Haworth Press.

Burke, P. (1997). *Gender shock: Exploding the myths of male and female,* New York: Anchor.

Chong, J.M.L. (1990). Social assessments of transsexuals who apply for sex reassignment therapy. *Social Work in Health Care, 14*(3), 87-105.

Council on Social Work Education. (1992). *Curriculum policy statement for master's degree programs in social work education.* Alexandria, VA: Council on Social Work Education.

De Jong, P., & Miller, S. D. (1995). How to interview for client strength. *Social Work, 40*(6), 729-736.

Erikson, E. (1950). *Childhood and society.* New York: W.W. Norton & Co.

Ettner, R. (1996). *Confessions of a gender defender: A psychologist's reflections on life among the transgendered.* Chicago: Evanston.

Ettner, R., & Brown, G.R. (1999). *Gender loving care: A guide to counseling gender-variant clients.* New York: W.W. Norton.

Feinberg, L. (1993). *Stone butch blues.* Ithaca, NY: Firebrand Books.

Feinberg, L. (1996). *Transgender warriors: Making history from Joan of Arc to Dennis Rodman.* Boston: Beacon Press.

Garnets, L., Hancock, K.A., Cochran, S. D., Goodchilds, J., & Peplau, L. A. (1991). Issues in psychotherapy with lesbians and gay men: A survey of psychologists. *American Psychologist, 46,* 964-972.

Gartrell, N. K. (1994). Boundaries in lesbian therapist-client relationships. In B. Greene & G.M. Herek (Eds.), *Lesbian and gay psychology: Theory, research, and clinical applications* (pp. 98-117). Thousand Oaks, CA: Sage Publications.

Germain, C. B. (1991). *Human behavior and the social environment.* New York: Columbia University Press.

Germain, C. B., & Gitterman, A. (1996). *The life model of social work practice* (2nd Ed.). New York: Columbia University Press.

Gochros, H. L. (1985). Teaching social workers to meet the needs of the homosexually oriented. In R. Schoenberg, R. Goldberg, and D. Shore (Eds.), *With compassion towards some: Homosexuality and social work in America* (pp. 137-156). New York: Harrington Park Press.

Gochros, H. (1995). Sex, AIDS, social work and me. *Reflections, 1*(2), 37-43.

Goffman, E. (1963). *Stigma: Notes of the management of a spoiled identity.* Englewood Cliffs, NJ: Prentice-Hall.

Goldberg, C. (1999, June 11). Issues of gender, from pronouns to murder. *The New York Times,* p. B2

Green, R. (1985). Gender identity in childhood and later sexual orientation: Follow-up of 78 males. *American Journal of Psychiatry, 142,* 339-341.

Greene, B. (1994). Lesbian and gay sexual orientations: Implications for clinical training, practice and research. In B. Greene & G.M. Herek (Eds.), *Lesbian and gay psychology: Theory, research, and clinical applications* (pp. 1-24). Thousand Oaks, CA: Sage Publications.

Herek, G. M. (1990). The context of anti-gay violence: Notes on cultural psychological heterosexism. *Journal of Interpersonal Violence, 5*(3), 316-333.

Humphreys, G. E. (1983). Inclusion of content on homosexuality in the social work curriculum. *Journal of Social Work Education, 19*(1), 55-60.

Jackson, P.A., & Sullivan, G. (Eds.). Special Issue of the *Journal of Gay & Lesbian Social Services, 9*(2/3).

Kahn, T.J. (1990). The adolescent transsexual in a juvenile corrections institution: A case study. *Child and Youth Care Quarterly, 19*(1), 21-30.

Levine, C.O. (1978). Social work with transsexuals. *Social Casework, 59*(3), 167-174.

Lombardi, E.L. (1999). Integration within a transgender social network and its effect upon members' social and political activity. *Journal of Homosexuality, 37*(1), 109-126.

Lombardi, E.L., Wilchins, R.A., Priesing, D., & Malouf, D. (1998). Gender violence: Transgender experiences with violence and discrimination. American Sociological Association paper.

Mallon, G. P. (1992a). Gay and no place to go: Serving the needs of gay and lesbian youth in out-of-home care settings. *Child Welfare, 71*(6), 547-557.

Mallon, G.P. (Ed). (1998). *Foundations of social work practice with lesbian and gay persons.* New York: Haworth Press.

Marcia, J.E. (1980). Identity in adolescence. In J. Adelson (Ed.) *Handbook of adolescent psychiatry* (pp. 159-187). New York: John Wiley & Sons.

Mason-Schrock, D. (1996). Transsexual's narrative construction of the "true self." *Social Psychology Quarterly, 59*(3), 176-192.

Mattaini, M. (1995). Knowledge for practice. In C. Meyer & M. Mattaini (Eds.), *Foundations of social work practice* (pp. 59-85). Washington, DC: NASW.

McGowan, B. (1995, October 16). Personal communication.

Meyer, C. (1982). Issues in clinical social work: In search of a consensus. In P. Carloff (Ed.), *Treatment formulations and clinical social work* (pp. 19-26). Silver Spring, MD: NASW.

Moore, B. (1999, March). Proposed public and professional policies: Transgender issues/Gender identity issues. *NASW News,* p. 12-13.

Newman, B. S. (1989). Including curriculum content on lesbian and gay issues. *Journal of Social Work Education, 25*(3), 202-211.

Norton, J. (1997). "Brain says you're a girl, but I think you're a sissy boy": Cultural origins of transphobia. *Journal of Gay, Lesbian, and Bisexual Identity, 2*(2), 139-164.

Offer, D. (1980). Adolescent development: A normative perspective. In S.I. Greenspan & G.H. Pollock (Eds.), *The course of life, vol II: Latency, adolescence, and youth.* U.S. Department of Health and Human Services Publication No. (ADM) 80-999. Washington, D.C.

Offer, D., Ostrov, E., & Howard, K. (1981). *The adolescent: A psychological self portrait.* New York: Basic Books.

Oles, M.N. (1977). The transsexual client: A discussion of transsexualism and issues in psychotherapy. *American Journal of Orthopsychiatry, 47*(1), 66-74.

Park, P. (1998, November 5). Are you a gender psychopath? Finding common cause in the battles against homophobia and transgenderphobia. *Lesbian and Gay New York*, p. 16.

Parlee, M.B. (1996). Situated knowledge's of personal embodiment: Transgender activists' and psychological perspectives on "sex" and "gender." *Theory and Psychology, 6*(4), 625-645.

Pharr, S. (1988). *Homophobia: A weapon of sexism.* Little Rock, AK: Chardon Press.

Scholinski, D. (1997). *The last time I wore a dress.* New York: Riverhead.

Volcano, D.L., & Halberstam, J. (1999). *The drag king book.* London: Serpent's Tail.

Wicks, L.K. (1977). Transsexualism: A social work approach. *Health and Social Work, 2*(1), 179-193.

Wilchins, R.A. (1997). *Read my lips: Sexual subversion and the end of gender.* New York: Firebrand Books.

Williams, W. (1997). The transgender phenomenon: An overview from the Australian perspective. *Verereology, 10*(3), 147-149.

Zucker, K.J., & Bradley, S.J. (1995). *Gender identity disorder and psychosexual problems in children and adolescents.* New York: Guilford Press.

Ethical Issues
in the Mental Health Treatment
of Gender Dysphoric Adolescents

Stephanie Swann
Sarah E. Herbert

SUMMARY. This paper will focus on ethical dilemmas that arise in the treatment of adolescents with gender dysphoria. We will begin with a discussion of ethical and legal issues pertinent to the treatment of any adolescent, and then proceed to the gender dysphoric adolescent, since there is a great deal of overlap between the two areas. The authors review legal decisions, the existing data on adolescent decision-making, and ethical principles that may help the clinician in resolving some very complex situations. Utilizing case vignettes of three gender dysphoric adolescents, the authors provide a pragmatic illustration of the ethical dilemmas involved in evaluation and treatment of these youth. It is the authors' belief that treatment interventions should be based on respect for the adolescent's autonomy and confidentiality where he or she is deemed competent to make decisions. *[Article copies available for a fee from The Haworth Document Delivery Service: 1-800-342-9678. E-mail address: getinfo@haworthpressinc.com <Website: http://www.haworthpressinc.com>]*

KEYWORDS. Ethical, gender dysphoria, adolescents, decision making

INTRODUCTION

There has been little attention paid to gender dysphoric adolescents compared to that given to gender dysphoric children and transsexual

Stephanie Swann is a social worker in Atlanta, Georgia. Sarah E. Hebert is affiliated with Emory Healthcare, 1365 Clifton Road NE, Suite B1600, Atlanta, GA 30322.

[Haworth co-indexing entry note]: "Ethical Issues in the Mental Health Treatment of Gender Dysphoric Adolescents." Swann, Stephanie, and Sarah E. Herbert. Co-published simultaneously in *Journal of Gay & Lesbian Social Services* (Harrington Park Press, an imprint of The Haworth Press, Inc.) Vol. 10, No. 3/4, 1999, pp. 19-34; and: *Social Services with Transgendered Youth* (ed: Gerald P. Mallon) Harrington Park Press, an imprint of The Haworth Press, Inc., 1999, pp. 19-34. Single or multiple copies of this article are available for a fee from The Haworth Document Delivery Service [1-800-342-9678, 9:00 a.m. - 5:00 p.m. (EST). E-mail address: getinfo@haworthpressinc.com].

adults. Yet these adolescents may be suffering from isolation, shame, rejection, school refusal, depression, and suicidality. They may feel desperate enough to take hormones obtained on the street or engage in self-mutilation in attempts to further their cross-gender identification. These emotions and behaviors may bring them to the attention of mental health professionals and social service workers in a variety of settings. Significant issues may arise for the therapists if gender dysphoric adolescents wish to cross-dress, use opposite gendered pronouns, and participate in activities as their desired gender rather than their biological sex. This engenders difficult ethical discussions among mental health professionals, and requires thoughtful interventions.

This paper will focus on ethical dilemmas that arise in the treatment of adolescents with gender dysphoria. We will begin with a discussion of ethical and legal issues pertinent to the treatment of any adolescent, and then proceed to the gender dysphoric adolescent, since there is a great deal of overlap between the two areas. This discussion will review legal decisions (Weithorn, 1985), the existing data on adolescent decision-making, and ethical principles that may help the clinician in resolving some very complex situations. Three different theoretical approaches to treatment will be examined with attention paid to the guiding principles behind each approach. Case vignettes of three gender dysphoric adolescents will provide a pragmatic illustration of the ethical dilemmas involved in evaluation and treatment of these individuals. It is the authors' belief that treatment interventions should be based in respect for the adolescent's autonomy and confidentiality where he or she is deemed competent to make decisions.

ETHICAL ISSUES
AND LEGAL DECISIONS INVOLVING MINORS

Issues of autonomy, confidentiality, and competence arise in the treatment of adolescent clients (Gustafson & McNamara, 1987). The clinician faced with complex questions involving adolescents may seek clarification through the law or professional codes of ethics. Legally, under most circumstances, it is parents who must give consent for their minor child, even if adolescent, to receive medical care. Children have been traditionally seen as the property of their parents or guardians, and these individuals were responsible for protecting them and providing for their care (Enzer, 1985; Grisso & Vierling, 1978).

Despite this, legal decisions in the past 20 years have given increasing recognition to the independence of adolescents to consent to their own medical treatment (Grisso & Vierling, 1978). Statutory laws in many states have defined specific conditions including venereal disease, pregnancy, and substance abuse which define adolescents as emancipated minors, and thus allow them to consent to their own medical treatment (Holder, 1996). Common law uses a "mature minor" exception to the requirement for parental consent for treatment. Under this principle in common law, young people may be judged to be mature enough to make medical decisions for themselves if they are old enough, understand the nature of a proposed treatment and its risks, can give the same degree of informed consent as an adult client, and if the treatment does not involve very serious risks (Holder, 1996). However, legal decisions and statutes that have been enacted may vary from state to state, and at times be contradictory.

Research on adolescent decision-making processes suggests that the abilities of adolescents in their mid to late teenage years are much closer to those of adults, even though they lack some of the life experiences (Mann, Harmoni, & Power, 1989). The ability to make a reasonable decision is one of the hallmarks of a mature adolescent. Tancredi (1982) defined competence as the "capacity to make rational or intelligent judgment." Embedded in competence is the ability to survey a wide range of alternative solutions, evaluate the positives and negatives of each possible consequence stemming from the options identified, incorporate new information from reliable sources even when it is offensive, and effectively implement the determined choice of action. It is assumed that the more adequately each of these steps is implemented, the more competent the decision-maker is (Mann, Harmoni, & Power, 1989).

Ethical codes for various professional organizations are quite general, and do not always address the specific issue that is of concern to the clinician. The Code of Ethics of the American Academy of Child Psychiatry (1980) states, "The formal responsibility for decisions regarding such participation (in evaluation, treatment or prevention involving a minor) usually resides with the parents or legal guardians" (p. 4). The American Psychological Association Code of Ethics states that psychologists "working with minors or other persons who are unable to give voluntary, informed consent . . . [are obliged to] take special care to protect these persons' best interests" (Sobocinski,

1990, p. 242). Both Codes of Ethics would suggest that minors are unable to give voluntary, informed consent. There are no references to the treatment of children and adolescents in the National Association of Social Workers Code of Ethics (NASW, 1996).

There are, as we will discuss next, complex therapeutic situations for which the clinician may not find a clear answer from the law or professional codes of ethics. In these circumstances, it may be helpful to refer to the more fundamental, abstract level of ethical decision-making using the ethical principles which are the foundation of the professional codes of ethics (Sobicinski, 1990). The ethical principles of respect for autonomy, beneficence, non-maleficence, and confidentiality are relevant to decision-making in these situations.

Respect for autonomy is the ethical principle which involves acknowledging an individual's "right to hold views, to make choices, and to take actions based on personal values and beliefs" (Beauchamp & Childress, 1994, p. 125). Respecting autonomy involves not just an attitude of respect, but respectful action. It involves treating persons to enable them to act autonomously, and not engaging in actions that ignore, insult, or demean them. It is based on recognition of the unconditional worth of all individuals, and the ability of them to determine their own destiny (Beauchamp & Childress, 1994).

The ethical principle of beneficence "refers to a moral obligation to act for the benefit of others" (Beauchamp & Childress, 1994, p. 260). Beneficence, has been defined as promoting good and removing harm, often translated into the best interests concept. It may be invoked when it is felt that an individual's autonomy should not be respected due to impairment in decision-making capacity. The individual's age, immaturity, cognitive impairment, and inability to reason rationally are all reasons given for not respecting the person's autonomy.

Non-maleficence is an ethical principle which "asserts an obligation not to inflict harm intentionally" (Beauchamp & Childress, 1994, p. 189). This principle is often invoked in discussions that focus on intending, causing, or permitting death to occur. However, it can also include harm involving the person's psychological or physical health in issues other than death.

Confidentiality is a concept involving the relationship between a professional and his or her client. It involves safeguarding and holding in trust disclosed information. Confidentiality "is present when the person to whom the information is disclosed pledges not to divulge that information to a third party without the confider's permission" (Beauchamp & Childress, 1994, p. 420). Implementation of this concept is limited by constraints of the law, and by situations where there is significant concern about danger to the individual or others. Clearly, confidentiality is an issue that comes up frequently in treating adolescents.

ETHICAL ISSUES IN TREATING GENDER DYSPHORIC ADOLESCENTS

These same issues of confidentiality, competence to make decisions, and conflict between the ethical principles of respect for autonomy and beneficence arise in the treatment of gender dysphoric adolescents. As clinicians, we may be confronted with what the limits of confidentiality are with respect to issues around gender identity. If a particular adolescent has significant concerns about his or her gender identity, discloses this in the therapy session, and wants assurance from the clinician that his or her parents won't be told, the clinician will be faced with the question of what his or her responsibility is in this matter. Issues of autonomy arise when parental or psychiatric definitions of healthy gender identity development come into direct conflict with the identity and goals of the gender dysphoric adolescent. Should parents and/or mental health clinicians dictate what the adolescent's gender identity should be, and set the goals of treatment to achieve this? If parents feel the most beneficent course of action is to involve the adolescent in psychiatric treatment, and not permit any expression of cross-gender behavior, should their decision be respected? If and when should the adolescent be able to participate in determining the goals of treatment? Can the gender dysphoric adolescent be treated as a competent individual whose autonomy is respected? For example, if a particular adolescent wishes to express his or her cross-gender identification at school or in a residential treatment center, should this be honored? Finally, questions arise concerning the adolescent's competence to consent to the significant decisions regarding hormone therapy, or surgical procedures such as breast implants or genital reconstruction.

THEORETICAL APPROACHES TO THE TREATMENT OF THE GENDER DYSPHORIC ADOLESCENT

There are several different theoretical approaches to the treatment of gender dysphoric adolescents. The first of these approaches is therapeutic intervention that is geared toward altering the adolescent's gender identity to be congruent with the biological sex. The second approach is supportive psychotherapy, an intervention that strives to alleviate intrapsychic distress while allowing the adolescent to continue to mature into adulthood. The third and final approach discussed is an intervention that not only provides ego support but also recognizes the role of social and cultural values. It addresses the manner in which society polarizes gender, and draws attention to the ways in which gender dysphoric adolescents are marginalized and pathologized for not conforming to norms of our culture. This approach is centered on the belief that the desired gender identification is a viable one. Therapeutic interventions may include facilitating the cross-gender transition, as well as assuming an active role in determining appropriateness for hormone therapy, and eventually sex reassignment surgery.

Historically, psychoanalytic psychotherapy and behavior therapy have both utilized the first approach of trying to alter the adolescent's cross-gender identification to be congruent with his or her biological sex. The focus of psychoanalytically-oriented treatment is the intrapsychic conflict that is assumed to be responsible for the gender dysphoria. The goal in behavioral interventions is the modification or elimination of specific characteristics and behaviors. Efforts to change an adolescent's gender identity have not been proven to be effective, with a few exceptions (Zucker & Bradley, 1995).

The second theoretical approach, supportive psychotherapy, uses several therapeutic interventions, including individual psychotherapy, family therapy, and case management in an attempt to alleviate psychological distress and strengthen ego functioning. Primary to this approach is the belief that decisions regarding core gender should be made when the adolescent reaches adulthood. The clinician attempts to facilitate the adolescent's exploration of his or her conflict between biological sex and gender identity while assessing sexual orientation and the possible confusion between gender and sexual orientation.

Gender dysphoric adolescents are reported to often present with comorbid personality disorders as well as other psychiatric difficulties such as poor frustration tolerance, increased anxiety, depression, substance abuse, and suicidality. Their cross-dressing behaviors have traditionally been viewed as a defensive solution to the anxiety that is experienced as intolerable (Zucker & Bradley, 1995). Supportive psychotherapy therefore places less emphasis on exploration as an aspect of facilitating the gender transition and instead attends to the management of the psychopathology in order for the adolescent to exist in his or her environment with the least amount of dysfunction. Resolution of the cross-gender identification with either a heterosexual or homosexual orientation is seen as the most successful outcome of therapy in this approach (Bradley & Zucker, 1997).

In a third treatment approach, the ultimate success is not thought of as a heterosexual or homosexual orientation, but instead the adolescent's gender dysphoric or transgender identification is viewed as a viable outcome. The therapist acknowledges the constraints and demands of society with regard to gender identity, and the impact this has on the complete development of the gender dysphoric adolescent. This approach is often best suited for the patient who has a childhood history of cross-gender identification that has persisted into the adolescent years.

The parents or guardians are often in need of support and education as they come to terms with their adolescent's desired gender identity and the fact that the cross-gender identification does not appear to be a transient phenomenon. The parents may have conflicted feelings about what it means to support their child in this process, and the possible consequences if they do so. If the adolescent has not begun to cross dress in his or her daily life, the therapist may be needed for guidance as the adolescent confronts the difficult consequences of beginning to live as the desired gender in the same community where he or she has previously lived. Often the adolescent has already begun to express visibly his or her cross-gender identification. If this is so, he or she may already be facing ostracism, harassment, and violence. In this case, it may be necessary for the clinician to advocate for the student within the school system, or assist in transfer to a new school. If appropriate, referral for further evaluation for hormone therapy may be undertaken.

Regardless of the theoretical approach to treatment, it is critical that we as clinicians working with gender dysphoric adolescents remain aware of our countertransference, and the ways in which our own biases may have an impact on the treatment. Ethical issues arise when the belief systems of the clinician, parents, and adolescent come into conflict. Belief systems incorporate not only professional knowledge, but also personal values, religious beliefs, and moral attitudes. Historically, our society has had explicit and implicit rules governing gender and gender role expression. An adolescent whose presentation is out of the realm of what has been defined as acceptable is likely to induce negative feelings for many clinicians thereby triggering messages from our individual belief systems. Even if this is not the case, awareness of society's expectations has an impact on our formulation of the problem, the intervention, and the desired solution. This awareness coupled with our own belief systems will contribute to the choice of ethical principles that guide our practice, and help us treat the gender dysphoric adolescent in the most therapeutic manner.

Next, case vignettes of three gender dysphoric adolescents will be utilized to illustrate the difficult ethical dilemmas faced by clinicians attempting to treat these individuals and their families.

CASE EXAMPLES

Case #1

Issues of confidentiality were posed by Faheed, a 15-year-old boy brought for evaluation because of what his mother called "sexual identity concerns." His chief complaint was "I never felt attracted to girls before." He had made two suicide attempts prior to being seen, and when questioned by his mother for the reason, he disclosed that he was very depressed because he was only attracted to same-sex individuals. However, when interviewed separately from his mother at the initial evaluation session he also stated, "I think of myself as a woman, not as gay." He reported that he disliked his body, giving as an example how he never wanted to go without a shirt in the summer the way other boys did. He hated dressing out for gym and refused to shower around other boys. Sexually, he acknowledged responsiveness to same-sex individuals, but said he didn't touch his genitals, nor did he allow others to touch them. He had had one previous sexual experience in which he had performed oral sex on a man he had casually met in another city when his family was there for vacation. His mother did not report any history of early cross-dressing or other evidence of cross-gender identification, but did describe him as a very sensitive and caring child.

The family was from an East Asian country, and their religion was Muslim. The patient was well aware that homosexuality was absolutely forbidden by his religion, and his parents had told him the penalty for being caught could be death. He said he would like to consider sex reassignment surgery if it weren't for his religion, which forbade any surgical intervention to alter the body.

Faheed was very concerned about the effect of his disclosure about his sexual orientation on his family, and did not want his parents to be told that he had any concerns about his gender identity. This posed an ethical dilemma for the treating psychiatrist. Should she respect this patient's request for confidentiality, and not disclose information regarding his gender identity concerns to his parents? Codes of ethics, when they comment on minors, generally suggest respecting a minor's confidentiality unless a situation of dangerousness to self or others exists. It was not felt that this individual's concerns regarding his gender identity were putting him or others in danger. He was not reporting suicidality, nor was he engaged in any behaviors at that time, sexual or otherwise, that could have put him at risk. What he appeared to need was a place where he could be free to discuss his emerging sexuality. Not respecting his desire for confidentiality would likely have disrupted this process. Since the cross-gender identification reported by Faheed followed his initial description of being attracted to same-sex peers, one consideration was that his internal conflict regarding homosexuality was leading him to consider being transsexual.

Faheed felt alone and isolated in the peer group at his school, and expressed a strong desire to meet other youth with concerns similar to his own. This presented another dilemma for the clinician. Awareness of the dearth of peer support in his current environment coupled with an understanding of the crucial role that a peer group plays in an adolescent's identity formation and consolidation led the psychiatrist to consider referral to a community support group and a helpline for gay, lesbian, and bisexual youth in addition to his individual therapy. The question was whether to inform both Faheed and his parents of these resources. If the parents were informed, it was felt that their strong religious beliefs would interfere with him attending the group, or even being allowed to continue in therapy.

A decision was made to inform Faheed of the possible community resources, and let him decide about informing his parents. The treating clinician felt that this young man was mature enough that his autonomy could be respected, and he could be allowed to make the decision about whether to inform his parents about these resources. The principle of beneficence, however, guided the psychiatrist to discuss with

Faheed the possible consequences of being rejected or further alienated from his family if he were to be more overt about socializing with his gay and lesbian peers, given his continued need to depend on his family.

Case #2

In the next case, issues of confidentiality, beneficence, and autonomy, including criteria for competent decision-making, are explored in greater depth. David was a 15-year-old African American biological male who was referred for outpatient psychotherapy following a brief inpatient psychiatric admission due to a suicidal gesture in which he ingested a mixture of household cleaning solutions. He immediately reported the incident to his high school counselor at which time he was hospitalized. He began weekly psychotherapy with complaints that included discomfort with his gender identity, depression, and a history of school refusal due to the violence and harassment he had experienced in that setting. This was the only treatment David had ever received with the exception of several sessions with a psychotherapist at age 10 for an inability to make friends, and withdrawn behaviors in the classroom. His biological mother, with whom he was living, also began her own individual therapy. Shortly after the initial assessment, David turned sixteen and subsequently dropped out of school and began cross-dressing daily. David's depressive symptoms resolved and he no longer reported suicidal ideation after he began cross-dressing, dropped out of school, and established a peer group through a local gay and lesbian youth organization.

David reported he had wanted to be a girl for as long as he could remember, but his mother denied any knowledge of this. She did, however, admit that David had frequently been mistaken for a girl since the age of two years. She confirmed that David had experienced a great deal of harassment and subsequent alienation from his peers due to his persistent feminine mannerisms and behaviors. David acknowledged attraction to same-sex peers from the age of thirteen, but did not consider himself a gay male.

Ambivalence in his gender identity was observed as David displayed an incongruence between his cross-dressing behavior and his continued use of his male name. Although David was able to pass, this incongruence between name and appearance was resulting in life problems, such as an inability to acquire a job and harassment from strangers to whom he frequently introduced himself and with whom he attempted to interact as he traveled the city via public transportation.

Over the course of treatment, David's cross-dressing became more seductive and more provocative. He discussed being frustrated by not having a job, but he denied any form of solicitation or prostitution. He did, however, report incidents of being propositioned and harassed while walking alone in an area of the city known for prostitution during late night hours. When he was confronted with the risks of his behavior and the danger he was placing himself in, David minimized the severity of the situation and rationalized his behavior. He stated that he had to spend time with his friends, he could do so only late at night, and that there was no public transportation after 11 PM, therefore leaving him no alternative but to walk home. His therapist suspected that David was not telling the truth, and in fact, was possibly engaging in prostitution.

Due to David's inability to effectively generate alternatives that would provide him with greater safety, and his unwillingness to discontinue the behavior, it became necessary at that point to elicit the support of his mother. David informed the therapist that he did not want his mother to know how late he was staying out, or that he had encountered any danger in doing so. He feared that if his mother was aware of his behaviors, she would ground him, and refuse to allow him to hang out with his new friends. He was insistent that he have the freedom to choose his own way of living. He threatened that if his mother attempted to stop him from cross-dressing or seeing his friends, he felt he would have no alternative but to run away from home. David had a history of running away, but had not done so for approximately one year, a time period coinciding with the beginning of his therapy. Was David competent to make his own decisions regarding treatment at this point?

At first glance, David, at age 16 and of average intelligence, might be an adolescent who would be thought of as a competent decision-maker. However, his poor judgment, lack of insight, and impulsivity made it necessary for the therapist to place the ethical principle of beneficence above the principle of respect for his autonomy and self-determination. This was accomplished by requesting that David's mother enter the treatment process thereby usurping his right to formulate his own treatment plan. It also became necessary to violate his confidentiality to the extent that was needed to provide him with the safety that he was unable to provide for himself.

The ethical conflicts involved in the decision to override David's autonomous decision-making and violate his confidentiality were further complicated by the therapist's hesitance to disrupt the therapeutic alliance with her client. Involving his mother and violating his confidentiality diminished the trust, and threatened the continuation of his therapy. The therapy provided a place where he could explore his cross-gender identification in a safer setting than that afforded to him on the streets. The therapist was concerned that he might resume his runaway behaviors, thus placing himself at further risk of being harmed. This was particularly worrisome given the improvement in his psychiatric symptoms and stability of his living situation that had taken place in the year he had been in therapy. The life-threatening consequences of respecting his autonomous decision-making in this case forced the clinician to take a more paternalistic stance despite the risk of negatively impacting the therapeutic relationship.

Case #3

Questions regarding respect for patient autonomy and competence to consent for treatment were handled differently by the clinician treating Daniel, an 18-year-old Caucasian biological male who was initially seen for evaluation when he was 16.5 years old. His mother, Mrs. M., requested a consultation to clarify his diagnosis. The psychologist who had been seeing Daniel felt that he was homosexual, yet Daniel did not agree with this, and Mrs. M. wanted another opinion to know if Daniel was transsexual. A month-and-a-half prior to being seen, he had dropped out of school because of persistent taunting by peers due to his femininity, and had begun cross-dressing full-time. He had attended a support group for gay, lesbian, and bisexual adolescents on one occasion at his mother's urging, but did not feel this group reflected how he saw himself. At the initial interview he commented, "I think I'm transsexual; I feel so much more natural dressing like this."

Mrs. M. had been seeking help regarding Daniel's cross-gender identification since he was three years old. Daniel's mother acknowledged wanting a girl for her second child, but did not feel she had treated Daniel any differently than his brother. As early as age two-and-a-half Daniel would try to wear high heels, and would put dishtowels on his head to simulate long hair. At age four he told his girlfriend to call him by a female name, and told people that he wanted to be a girl. Toy interests were for feminine ones such as "My Little Pony," where he could spend time combing the pony's long mane and tail, and Mrs. M. described how he took the role of mother when playing house. Until fifth grade, his mother reported that his feminine gender role behaviors were more overt, but that they diminished after this point. Daniel said the gender issues were present, but he learned by fifth grade not to talk about his desire to be female.

Since the age of ten, Daniel has been aware of an attraction to same-sex peers. In an effort to explore his sexuality, he became involved in some telephone sex in early adolescence, and then in mid-adolescence met men and performed oral sex when cross-dressed several times, apparently in both situations passing as a woman. In his first sexual interaction at age 13, and in all subsequent ones, he has never allowed a partner to touch his penis through masturbation or oral sex. He has performed oral sex, and been penetrated himself in anal intercourse. At the time of the initial assessment, Daniel had a 16-year-old boy-friend who apparently had not known he was a biological male until he disclosed this after they had been seeing each other a short time. Daniel said his only friends were straight girls at the school he had attended. He remarked that there were few guys who were willing to be seen around him.

Mrs. M. had initially sought consultation about her son's atypical gender role behaviors when he was three years old. Family counseling had been recommended at that time, but the family did not follow through on this recommendation. However, Daniel was in therapy from ages four-and-a-half to six-and-a-half years with another psychologist, apparently to help him in coping with the parents' divorce, but also with gender identity issues. Mrs. M. sought consultation with the chief of child psychiatry at a local medical school around this same time. He said he could give no final opinion, that it would take time to determine what the outcome would be, and his recommendation was for Daniel to continue in therapy. During this time, his mother reports doing as much as possible to offer more stereotypically masculine toys, to reinforce more masculine gender role behaviors, to find activities in which he could participate with other boys. Daniel remembers being offered a Mickey Mouse watch he desperately wanted if he would act in less feminine ways; he reports doing so just long enough to get the watch and then reverted to his previous ways of behaving. In fifth grade, he began weekly therapy with the psychologist he had been seeing for six years at the time he came for evaluation.

It was clear that Daniel had had a long-standing gender identity disorder which had not abated with time, with multiple attempts at psychotherapy, and behavioral intervention, and that a transsexual resolution was becoming obvious. Prior to the consultation, he had decided on his own that he could no longer tolerate going to school and living as a male, and began cross-dressing full-time. Daniel understood the consequences of this, but did not feel he could continue to handle the harassment he had been experiencing in the school setting. At the time of the consultation, Daniel expressed a desire to begin hormone therapy as soon as possible. He knew the longer he waited to begin, the more his body would show the masculinization, which caused him so much distress. Mrs. M. made it clear that she and Daniel's father were willing to consider this. The risks and the benefits of hormone therapy were discussed with Daniel on his own, and with his mother present. He was able to grasp this information, and understood that some of the changes such as the development of breast tissue might not be reversible should he want to change his mind. Daniel understood that the professionals treating him might worry that he would change his mind, but articulated a strong belief that this was what was right for him. Daniel was referred for consultation to a local endocrinologist, who began hormone therapy shortly after this evaluation at age 16.5 years of age.

Since the time of the initial evaluation, Daniel has asked family, friends, and treating clinicians to use female pronouns and the female name selected in the legal name change. At this point in the case, the female pronoun will now be used, and Daniel referred to as Danielle. Danielle has consistently taken the hormone therapy prescribed by her endocrinologist, she has lived as a female, had a legal name change, and had a series of jobs where she has successfully passed as female. She continues to ruminate about what she sees as "boy features" when she looks in the mirror, but overall is making a positive adaptation. She has difficulty maintaining a job, not because of having trouble passing, but because of conflicts that arise with her supervisors. After recently turning eighteen she received breast implants, and has continued to work toward her goal of sex reassignment surgery.

The psychiatrist in this case has provided referral information and consultation with the other physicians treating Danielle during this time of gender transition.

Respect for autonomy is an ethical principle that acknowledges an individual's right to hold views, make choices, and take actions based on that individual's values and beliefs (Beauchamp & Childress, 1994). Choices made by an autonomous individual rest on the assumption that the person is competent. The dilemma in adolescence is one cannot assume that adolescents are fully competent in all areas of their lives. To deny that they have any competence to make decisions, however, is likewise unjustified (Sobicinski, 1990). A review of articles that are pertinent to the subject of minors and informed consent suggests that older adolescents do have decision-making capacity that is comparable to that of adults. In fact, some authors have suggested there are no psychological grounds on which to deny adolescents fifteen years and older the option of giving informed consent for their medical treatment and the decisions that entails. Piaget's theory of cognitive development would suggest that once an adolescent has achieved formal operations, he or she has a better ability to conceptualize future consequences of decisions made.

In order to give informed consent, the following criteria must be met: the consent is truly voluntary, there is adequate disclosure of information, there is comprehension of this information, and the person is competent to decide. Danielle's psychiatrist felt that she was able to understand the risks and benefits of pursuing her goal of sex reassignment surgery. She was able to articulate the risks and benefits of hormone therapy, and was also able to discuss the risks and benefits of not getting treatment until age 18. There was no one pressuring Danielle to go ahead, and thus her consent was voluntary. Her decision-making capacity was felt to be adequate for giving informed consent for hormone therapy. Danielle's autonomy was respected by her mother, and treating physicians, as it was felt that she was competent to make these decisions, and give informed consent.

CONCLUSION

In conclusion, ethical dilemmas arise in the treatment of gender dysphoric adolescents. As social workers and mental health professionals, we may face situations in which we are asked to answer complex questions for which there is no obviously correct or easy answer. What we can know is that these adolescents are individuals whose struggles with cross-gender identification need to be listened to and responded to with respect and sensitivity. No longer is it acceptable to equate gender dysphoria or transgender identification with severe psychopathology. This affects not only the way we formulate our understanding of the gender dysphoric adolescent, but also the theoretical approach to treatment and the way in which we resolve ethical dilemmas.

REFERENCES

American Academy of Child and Adolescent Psychiatry. (1980). *Code of ethics.* Washington, DC: Author.

Beauchamp, T.L., & Childress, J.F. (1994). *Principles of biomedical ethics* (4th Ed.) New York: Oxford University Press.

Bradley, S.J., & Zucker, K.J. (1997). Gender identity disorder: A review of the past ten years. *Journal of the American Academy of Child & Adolescent Psychiatry, 36,* 872-880.

Enzer, N.B. (1985). Ethics in child psychiatry–an overview. In D.H. Schetky & E.P. Benedek (Eds.), *Emerging issues in child psychiatry and the law* (pp. 3-21). New York: Brunner/Mazel Inc.

Grisso, T., & Vierling, L. (1978). Minors' consent to treatment: A developmental perspective. *Professional Psychology, 9,* 412-427.

Gustafson, K.E., & McNamara, J.R. (1987). Confidentiality with minor clients: Issues and guidelines for therapists. *Professional Psychology: Research and Practice, 18,* 503-508.

Holder, A.R. (1996). Legal issues in professional liability. In M. Lewis (Ed.), *Child and adolescent psychiatry: A comprehensive textbook* (2nd ed.). Baltimore, MD: Williams and Williams.

Mann, L., Harmoni, R., & Power, C. (1989). Adolescent decision-making: The development of competence. *Journal of Adolescence, 12,* 265-278.

National Association of Social Workers. (1996). Code of Ethics. Washington, DC, NASW Press.

Newman, L.E. (1970). Transsexualism in adolescence: Problems in evaluation and treatment. *Archive of General Psychiatry, 23,* 112-121.

Sobocinski, M.R. (1990). Ethical principles in the counseling of gay and lesbian adolescents: Issues of autonomy, competence, and confidentiality. *Professional Psychology: Research and Practice, 21,* 240-247.

Standards of Care: The hormonal and surgical sex reassignment of gender dysphoric persons (1985). *Archive of Sexual Behavior, 14,* 79-90.

Weithorn, L.A. (1985). Children's capacities for participation in treatment decision-making. In D.H. Schetky & E.P. Benedek (Eds.), *Emerging Issues in Child Psychiatry and the Law* (pp. 22-35). New York: Brunner/Mazel.

Zucker, K.J., & Bradley, S.J. (1995). Gender identity disorder and psychosexual problems in children and adolescents. New York: Guilford Press.

Internal and External Stress Factors Associated with the Identity Development of Transgendered Youth

Christian Burgess

SUMMARY. The goal of this paper is to present an alternative to a traditionally-held view that transgendered youth suffer from some sort of disorder, and instead shed light on the internal and external stress factors that may lead the young person to seek help. Social service professionals need to be aware of such factors in order to make a full assessment of what a potential transgendered adolescent client's issues are, and in order to work at changing some of these external pressures societally so that more transgendered youth can attain peaceful identity integration. *[Article copies available for a fee from The Haworth Document Delivery Service: 1-800-342-9678. E-mail address: getinfo@haworthpressinc.com <Website: http://www.haworthpressinc.com>]*

KEYWORDS. Transgendered youth, identity issues, trans-affirming social services

INTRODUCTION

Transgendered youth are among the most neglected, misunderstood groups in our society today. In addition to undergoing the regular perils of adolescence, these young people face an extraordinary

---

Christian Burgess is a graduate of Hunter College School of Social Work in New York City.

[Haworth co-indexing entry note]: "Internal and External Stress Factors Associated with the Identity Development of Transgendered Youth." Burgess, Christian. Co-published simultaneously in *Journal of Gay & Lesbian Social Services* (Harrington Park Press, an imprint of The Haworth Press, Inc.) Vol. 10, No. 3/4, 1999, pp. 35-47; and: *Social Services with Transgendered Youth* (ed: Gerald P. Mallon) Harrington Park Press, an imprint of The Haworth Press, Inc., 1999, pp. 35-47. Single or multiple copies of this article are available for a fee from The Haworth Document Delivery Service [1-800-342-9678, 9:00 a.m. - 5:00 p.m. (EST). E-mail address: getinfo@haworthpressinc.com].

amount of additional internal and external pressures associated with their identity development, centered around a society that is over-whelmingly uncomfortable with gender non-conformity. When left unchecked, these pressures amount to extreme isolation and confu-sion, which can lead to an array of bio-psycho-social problems, from substance abuse to self-mutilation.

No exact numbers are known regarding the prevalence of self-iden-tified transgendered individuals in this or other countries. This is perhaps due to the broad scope that the label "transgender" encom-passes. In the early 1990s, different communities of gender-variant individuals began to unite politically and socially to demand the rights and respect they deserved. These communities include cross-dressers, drag kings/queens, transsexuals, transgenderists, gender-benders, masculine women, feminine men, androgynes, etc. The word "trans-gender" then emerged to unite these groups under an umbrella term that includes all of those who challenge the boundaries of sex and gender (Carranante, 1999; Feinberg, 1996).

Given this definition, it is appropriate to make the assumption that the transgender community, while small compared to the overall popu-lation, is still a large and significant one. This is reflected within the population of adolescents as well. As the transgender community gains more visibility within societal institutions, especially the media, more and more young people are becoming comfortable in asserting their gender non-conforming characteristics.

Concurrently, with increased visibility comes an increase in backlash. Families, schools, peer groups, places of employment and other institu-tions are often ignorant or ill-equipped with accurate knowledge of this population, and as a result isolate these young people or ignore them altogether. To help stem this problem, it is up to social service agencies and human service professionals to work with transgender youth in eas-ing the isolation and confusion, and in bridging the gaps between them-selves and their families, schools, peers and other social systems.

The goal of this paper is to present an alternative to a traditionally-held view that transgender youth suffer from some sort of disorder, and instead shed light on the external factors that may lead the young person to seek help. Social service professionals need to be aware of such factors in order to make a full assessment of what a potential transgender adolescent client's issues are, and in order to work at changing some of these external pressures societally so that more transgender youth can attain peaceful identity integration.

REVIEW OF THE LITERATURE

There are no published books specifically on transgender youth. However, in recent years, there has been a proliferation of popular literature on the general topic of transgender issues. Leslie Feinberg (1996), Kate Bornstein (1994), Ricki Ann Wilchins (1997) and others have written extensively on the subject of transgender theory, culture and politics, but have by and large neglected mentioning issues specifically affecting transgender youth in their works. Despite the inclusion of transgender youth in agencies serving lesbian, gay and bisexual young people, the books focusing on these populations have failed to include transgender youth in their titles or in their content, with an occasional two-to-three pages on gender identity included but no more.

There is a similar paucity of information on the subject among academic and formal research. A search for literature using the keywords "transgender youth" within the Social Work Abstracts, Sociofile, and PsycLit research systems yielded no results. Even when using more clinical and outdated terms such as transsexual or Gender Identity Disorder when describing this community, results are minimal and, due to the clinical nature of the literature, limited in scope.

Much of the literature written about this community is punitive in nature, or contains language that pathologizes the group as a whole. Words such as "miserable," "troubled," and reference to an individual's transgender identity as a "problem" are common, and do not include differentiation between one's gender identity and other psychosocial issues that may be present (substance abuse, depression, etc.), or without mention of society's role in creating the distress within the individual (Lothstein, 1983; Steiner, 1985; Wicks, 1977). These attitudes and thoughts may be due to the popular thought of the time in which they were written, but nonetheless point to the need to revise and add to the current crop of academic literature, so that such negative references can be counterbalanced with accurate and unbiased reflections of this community.

The majority of literature regarding transgender youth specifically focuses on treatment of those within this community who identify or who are labeled as transsexuals, or who are diagnosed with Gender

Identity Disorder. Suggested treatment approaches run from forced behavioral modification during childhood and adolescence (Riseley, 1986; Zucker, 1985) to cognitive therapy emphasizing self-exploration and identity integration (Kahn, 1990; Levine, 1978).

No literature was found that simply paints an objective, descriptive account of the developmental aspects of transgender youth outside the clinical setting. This is significant because although information obtained from youth who seek treatment is valuable, it may be skewed if such accounts are taken to be representative of an entire population. The distinction between one's gender identity and mental health issues becomes blurred, and the result is often that the individual's gender identity is seen as the "problem"–the source of the adolescent's pain and confusion.

Fortunately, more literature is being written today that shifts the focus from the gender identity as the "problem" to the external factors that lead to internal distress. For transgender youth, the external factors are manifested most often through social pressures to conform to traditional gender expectations. These social pressures emanate from popular culture, families, schools, peer groups, social service agencies and other institutions that define society's culture. When an adolescent defies these expectations–to varying degrees and through a variety of means–confusion and isolation settle in that then lead to intra-psychic problems and behaviors such as depression, low self-esteem, substance abuse/hormonal abuse and self-mutilation, compounded by additional factors such as running away from/being kicked out of one's home, homelessness, prostitution, increased risk of exposure to STDs, dropping out of school and unemployment (Cohen, 1991; Denny, 1995; Galambos et al., 1990; Kahn, 1990; Rodgers, 1997; Ryan & Futterman, 1998).

Within the clinical community of psychiatrists, psychologists, and therapists, much of the dominant thought regarding transgenderists rests on the "condition" known as Gender Identity Disorder (GID). To gain an understanding of where these clinicians are coming from, and thus gain an understanding of the preponderance of literature on the subject, it is important to review this issue.

Gender Identity Disorder is a classification of the *Diagnostic and Statistical Manual of Mental Disorders*, Fourth Edition (American Psychiatric Association, 1994). The diagnostic criteria for GID are as follows:

A. A strong and persistent cross-gender identification (not merely a desire for any perceived cultural advantages of being the other sex).

In children, the disturbance is manifested by four (or more) of the following:

1. repeatedly stated desire to be, or insistence that he or she is, the other sex;
2. in boys, preference for cross-dressing or simulating female attire; in girls, insistence on wearing only stereotypically masculine clothing;
3. strong and persistent preferences for cross-sex roles in make believe play or persistent fantasies of being the other sex;
4. intense desire to participate in the stereotypical games and pastimes of the other sex;
5. strong preference for playmates of the other sex.

In adolescents and adults, the disturbance is manifested by symptoms such as a stated desire to be the other sex, frequent passing as the other sex, desire to live or be treated as the other sex, or the conviction that he or she has the typical feelings and reactions of the other sex.

B. Persistent discomfort with his or her sex or sense of inappropriateness in the gender role of that sex.

In children, the disturbance is manifested by any of the following: in boys, assertion that his penis or testes are disgusting or will disappear or aversion toward rough-and-tumble play and rejection of male stereotypical toys, games, and activities; in girls, rejection of urinating in a sitting position, assertion that she does not want to grow breasts or menstruate, or marked aversion toward normative feminine clothing.

In adolescents and adults, the disturbance is manifested by symptoms such as preoccupation with getting rid of primary and secondary sex characteristics (e.g., request for hormones, surgery, or other procedures to physically alter sexual characteristics to simulate the other sex) or belief that he or she was born the wrong sex.

C. The disturbance is not concurrent with a physical intersex condition.
D. The disturbance causes clinically significant distress or impairment in social, occupational, or other important areas of functioning (American Psychiatric Association, 1994).

There are many arguments against the GID classification: it is used as a subliminal means to diagnose homosexuality (and to subsequently try and "cure" it); it stigmatizes children, adolescents and adults who do not conform to traditional gender norms, even in the slightest way. In essence, opponents of the classification charge that it results in the diagnosis of a disorder that is in reality not present, creates a stigma around one's identity that leads to internalized shame, and in some cases, especially for children and adolescents, leads to forced treatments involving the imposition of gender norms (Osborne, 1997; Wilson, 1997).

Proponents of maintaining the classification argue that a GID diagnosis is necessary to satisfy requirements of the Harry Benjamin Standards of Care, a list of guidelines that candidates for sex reassignment surgery (SRS) must follow. Further, those in favor of keeping the classification say that it validates the experiences of those who are transgender (often called "gender dysphoric" in clinical circles) by giving practitioners a framework from which to operate (Osborne, 1997; Steiner, 1985).

Kathy Wilson (1997) from the Gender Identity Center of Colorado offers a solution to the debate: "It is possible to retain a diagnosis that specifically addresses the needs of the pre-operative transsexuals, requiring medical sex reassignment, with criteria that clearly and unambiguously exclude others for whom the diagnosis serves no therapeutic purpose." Wilson and others encourage clinicians to make a diagnosis on the basis of other psychosocial factors that may be present, such as depression, and multiple personality disorder.

PHYSICAL AND PSYCHOLOGICAL CHANGES

Adolescence is a time for great social, biological, and psychological changes. For almost all young people, this is a confusing time fraught with unexpected twists and turns. Perhaps the most intense changes come during puberty, when the body undergoes physical growth and sexual maturation. While many adolescents find solace in these changes through standard health curricula that teaches them what to expect and in peer groups where they can share stories of their physical trials and tribulations, transgender youth seldom have such support systems.

Puberty is often the time when transgender adolescents become the most confused and isolated. Where gender non-conformity in childhood may not have been taken as seriously by external systems, and the child may have been content with the idea that he or she would soon become the opposite sex, in adolescence those premonitions are shattered.

Physically, transgender youth may become repelled or ashamed of their developing sexual characteristics. They may begin to wear bulky clothing year-round to mask physical changes, and to use tight under-garments or bandages to bind breasts or genitals. In extreme cases, young people may also make attempts at removing unwanted sex organs through auto-castration or constant repeated pounding of breasts. Hormonal abuse may occur as well, with young people self-administering estrogen or testosterone supplements. Other attempts at altering physical appearance include injecting silicone in male-to-fe-male transgendered youth in their lips, chest, buttocks or thighs. For female-to-male youth, steroid abuse or the excessive use of powders meant for bodybuilding may be tried (Brown & Rounsely, 1996; Denny, 1995; Rodgers, 1997; Ryan & Futterman, 1998).

Psychological changes are also heightened for transgender youth. The mood swings and "testing of limits" through increased risk-tak-ing, typical in adolescence, may signify deeper trouble for these youth. Because of the internalization of negative attitudes toward gender non-conformity, transgender youth are at an increased risk for low self-esteem, which may manifest itself through depression, substance abuse, self-mutilation and/or suicide.

EXTERNAL PRESSURES

The biological and psychological distress of transgender youth is often symptomatic of pressures created from the macro and mezzo systems surrounding these young people. Pressures to conform to traditional gender norms intensify during adolescence and the degree of those expectations greatly shapes how the individual copes with the physical and psychological changes. Zastrow and Kirst-Ashman (1995) summarize the importance of these systems:

> Family and peer group mezzo systems are dynamically involved in childhood growth, development, and behavior. Social interac-tion with other people in childhood provides the foundation for building an adult social personality. Macro systems within the

environment, including communities, government units, and agencies, can provide necessary resources to help families address issues and solve problems typically experienced with children. Impinging macro systems within the social environment can act either to help or hinder family members fulfill their potential. (p. 144)

Family

The family is the system with perhaps the greatest influence on one's development. From birth through young adulthood, this unit has as one of its primary tasks the "physical, mental, emotional, and social development of each of its members" (Duvall, 1971). No matter what the makeup of the family, no matter what the cultural background, gender expectations are often strong and unswerving. Families often intervene during childhood if a child does not meet these expectations, through discipline or therapy, or they let the child push the boundaries with the presumption that the behavior is a phase.

If the child continues to express her/himself outside of gender expectations into adolescence, however, the interventions become more swift and severe. The expression of identity becomes an act of rebellion in the parent or guardian's eyes, which must be punished more severely or with more intense therapy. Parents or guardians take out their own discomfort with gender non-conformity on their child, resulting in strained relations and further isolation of the adolescent.

Of course, the degree of negative reaction usually corresponds with the degree of gender non-conformity. For instance, a parent's reaction to a male-to-female youth wearing black nail polish and having his ears pierced may not be the same as their reaction to a female-to-male youth wearing a tuxedo to the prom. These behaviors may still be viewed by the family as testing the limits and identity formation, and they may think the adolescent will still grow out of it, but as the adolescent gets older and/or as the behaviors and expressions of gender identity become more gender non-conforming, the parent or guardian may view the situation more seriously.

In the event of extreme and/or persistent gender non-conformity, or if youths, disclose to their parents that they are transgender, the family may react with extreme behaviors in turn. Physical, emotional and verbal abuse may occur, or the youth might be thrown out of the home.

Also, youths may become so isolated in the home as a result of the family's discomfort and shame that they run away.

Parents, Family and Friends of Lesbians and Gays (PFLAG), a national organization comprised of a network of local support and advocacy groups, has recently fostered initiatives to assist families with transgendered children in acquiring the knowledge and skills necessary to create a healthy environment in the home. In addition, more sensitive clinicians are encouraging families to allow adolescents to express their own gender identity, albeit with compromises (until the child is older), such as cross-dressing at home but not in public. Still, many families are unaware of such organizations or therapeutic techniques, and even so, are so entrenched with rigid gender roles that for transgender youth, the family is a system that more often than not fails to fulfill its roles as nurturer and caretaker.

Schools

After families, schools have the second most significant impact on one's development during adolescence. Schools are the testing ground for social skills, and through this testing, identity formation takes place. Fortunately, there are cliques where transgender youth may be accepted, and in some schools, cliques of lesbian, gay, bisexual and transgender youth are forming on their own, through clubs and informal friendship networks. Transgender youth are "coming out" in schools in increasing numbers, asserting their identity and demanding attention.

Despite these positive strides, school communities still have a long way to go. Curricula remain negligent of mentioning transgender issues, from historical figures to reading assignments to sexuality education. It is also rare that sensitivity training occurs among faculty and staff on the unique needs of transgender youth. Further, many rites of passage that occur within the context of schools are traumatic for transgender youth. Physical education, pressures to date, classes that track the specific sexes (shop for boys and home economics for girls, for instance), and the prom are all examples of middle and secondary school rituals that adhere to strict traditional gender norms. Teasing and harassment are also things that most transgender youth must endure, and can also take the form of violence. As with family, pressures at school lead to further isolation of transgender youth.

Other Systems

In addition to the family and school systems, other institutions also exert pressure on transgender youth to conform and suppress their identity. Health care professionals, employers, and places of worship are too often dead ends for these youth, offering no solace and more isolation. The social service agencies that transgender youth then turn to for help or to which they are referred through no choice of their own often continue the path of ignorance and neglect. Foster care and group homes, youth homeless shelters, juvenile detention centers and jails, community centers, after-school programs and other institutions are commonly just as ill-equipped at welcoming transgender youth as the institutions the youth are attempting to escape from (Robledo & Nish, 1999).

Safe Space

Exceptions do abound, though, and must be mentioned. Across the country, youth-service agencies that serve all youth and/or lesbian, gay and bisexual youth are becoming better equipped to address the unique needs of transgender youth, offering safe havens where they can "be themselves" free from persecution.

Streetwork is one such agency. Located in New York City, Streetwork is a program of Victim Services, a government agency that provides assistance to victims of violent crimes. The mission of the program includes "reaching out to the homeless and disenfranchised youth of Times Square (and other areas of New York), offering them respite from hunger, cold, loneliness and fear, and the opportunity to reclaim for themselves a sense of dignity and self-worth." In essence, the agency fills the void left by the families of many of these youth, many of whom identify as transgender.

Ines Robledo, the drop-in center coordinator for Streetwork, and David Nish, clinical director, state that the agency strives to provide alternatives for the youth to counteract the negative experiences they often encounter when accessing mainstream services. Healthcare and legal services are provided on-site, support and discussion groups are available, as well as safe and confidential counseling, social alternatives, and access to showers and food. A team of outreach workers also goes to the streets to provide services directly.

IMPLICATIONS FOR PRACTICE

It is in the interest of social service professionals to duplicate the efforts of agencies such as Streetwork. Social Workers are in the unique position to address the isolation and persecution of transgender youth from many angles.

A multi-systems approach needs to be utilized so that interventions can be developed that will address all of the institutions that affect the identity development of transgender youth. The American Psychiatric Association should be targeted to re-evaluate its current classification of Gender Identity Disorder. The lesbian, gay, and bisexual community should continue to strengthen its effort to include transgender individuals in its organizing efforts and agency services, and the transgender community should be pushed to be more aware of and inclusive of transgender youth. The organizing work of transgender youth themselves needs to gain more recognition and support from the above communities and the youth-services community, as these young people create their own groups, publications, and web-sites.

At the therapeutic level, clinicians must truly embrace the philosophy of "meeting clients where they are," by providing a safe space where transgender youth can express themselves and discuss their identity formation free from bias. Accurate information regarding the transgender community and issues affecting the transgender community, such as sex reassignment surgery (SRS) and hormones, should be available to youth. Such access to information may instill hope to frustrated transgender adolescents and deter them from mis-using hormones or altering their bodies using unsafe, harmful techniques. Support and discussion groups, the creation of social alternatives such as drop-in centers and access to positive role models are needed. All of these methods are vital steps in assisting with the formation of an integrated identity for transgender youth.

Above all else, the very core of what social service professionals can do is provide acceptance and positive affirmation for these youth. Just a simple validation of who the individual is, including his/her gender identity, can make all the difference in the world for that person. Acceptance will lead to a willingness to learn, the willingness to learn will lead to understanding, and understanding will lead to the eventual cessation of oppression and isolation of transgender youth.

AREAS FOR FURTHER STUDY

Because this is such an under-studied field, any additional research on the issues affecting transgender youth would be beneficial. Numerous topics would benefit from further scrutiny, such as transgender youth in the foster care system, on the streets, female-to-male transgender youth, etc. Comprehensive interviews and questionnaires administered to transgender youth would be an especially useful research tool, as no major studies have been undertaken to survey the needs and experiences of this population. The varied experience of transgender youth according to race and ethnicity is also an important area of study, as these variations are often overlooked in all subjects of research. Finally, studies that look at the long-term effects of various treatments would be useful to the debate over Gender Identity Disorder, and would help shape intervention approaches in general.

CONCLUSION

Transgendered youth deserve the attention of the social services community, for they have been neglected for far too long. This neglect has resulted in a group that is one of the most marginalized in our society, compounded by the extreme isolation and violence suffered from within their families, schools, and other social institutions. Some say that oppression based on sex and gender is at the root of all of our society's evils. If this is true, then it is surely our youth that are suffering the most, for it is often too difficult for them to speak for themselves. Social service professionals can help them find their voices, and become the wonderful transgendered individuals they are meant to be.

REFERENCES

American Psychiatric Association. (1994). *Diagnostic and statistic manual of mental disorders* (4th ed.). Washington, DC: Author.
Bornstein, K. (1994). *Gender outlaws: On men, women, and the rest of us.* New York: Routledge.
Brown, M.L., & Rounsley, C.A. (1996). *True selves: Understanding transsexualism.* San Francisco: Jossey-Bass Publishers.
Carranante, T. (1999). *Glossary of gender/transgender terms.* Unpublished document.

Cohen, Y. (1991). Gender identity conflicts in adolescents as motivation for suicide. *Adolescence, 26*(101), 19-29.

Denny, D. (1995). *Transgendered youth at risk for exploitation, HIV, hate crimes.* Unpublished manuscript, American Educational Gender Information Services, Inc.

Devor, H. (1997). *FTM: Female-to-male transsexuals in society.* Bloomington and Indianapolis: Indiana University Press.

Duvall, E. (1971). Cited from Schriver, J.M. (1995). *Human behavior in the social environment: Shifting paradigms in essential knowledge for social work practice.* Boston: Allyn and Bacon.

Feinberg, L. (1996). *Transgender warriors: Making history from Joan of Arc to Dennis Rodman.* Boston: Beacon Press.

Galambos, N.L., Almeida, D.M., & Petersen, A.C. (1990). *Masculinity, femininity, and sex role attitudes in early adolescence: Exploring gender intensification, 61,* 1905-1914.

Kahn, T.J. (1990). The adolescent transsexual in a juvenile corrections institution: A case study. *Child & Youth Care Quarterly, 19*(1), 21-29.

Levine, C.O. (1978). Social work with transsexuals. *Social Casework, 59*(3), 167-174.

Lothstein, L.M. (1983). *Female-to-male transsexualism.* Boston: Routledge & Kegan Paul.

Osborne, D. (1997). An attack on our most vulnerable: The use and abuse of gender identity disorder. *Lesbian and Gay New York,* October 28.

Riseley, D. (1986). Gender identity disorder of childhood: Diagnostic and treatment issues. In Walters, W.A.W., & Ross, M.W. (Eds.), *Transsexualism and sex reassignment* (pp. 26-43). New York: Oxford University Press.

Robledo, I., & Nish, D. (April 8, 1999). Personal interview.

Rodgers, L.L. (1997). Transgendered youth fact sheet. *Transgender protocol: Treatment services guidelines for substance abuse treatment providers* (2nd ed.). Unpublished report, Transgender Protocol Team of the San Francisco Lesbian, Gay, Bisexual, Transgender Substance Abuse Advisory Committee.

Ryan, C., & Futterman, D. (1998). *Lesbian and gay youth: Care and counseling.* New York: Columbia University Press.

Steiner, B.W. (Ed.). (1985). *Gender dysphoria: Development, research, management.* New York: Plenum Press.

Wicks, L.K. (1977). Transsexualism: A social work approach. *Health and Social Work, 2*(1), 180-193.

Wilchins, R.A. (1997). *Read my lips: Sexual subversion and the end of gender.* Ithaca: Firebrand Books.

Wilson, K. (1997). *Do cross-gender expression and identity constitute mental illness?* (On-line). Available: http://www.transgender.org/tg/gic/awptext.html#intro

Zastrow, C., & Kirst-Ashman, K.K. (1995). *Understanding human behavior and the social environment* (3rd ed.). Chicago: Nelson-Hall Publishers.

Zucker, K.J. (1985). Cross-gender identified children. In Steiner, B.W. (Ed.), *Gender dysphoria: Development, research and management.* New York: Plenum Press.

Practice with Transgendered Children

Gerald P. Mallon

SUMMARY. Utilizing an ecological framework and based on the existing literature and research, as well as my own 24 years of clinical practice with children, youth, and families, this paper examines gender variant childhood development from a holistic viewpoint where children and environments are understood as a unit, in the context of their relationship to one another. This chapter is limited to a discussion regarding the recognition of gender identity; an examination of the adaptation process through which gender variant children deal with the stress of an environment where there is not a "goodness of fit"; and a discussion of the overall developmental tasks of a transgendered childhood. Recommendations for social work practice with gender variant children are presented in the conclusion of the paper. *[Article copies available for a fee from The Haworth Document Delivery Service: 1-800-342-9678. E-mail address: getinfo@haworthpressinc.com <Website: http://www.haworthpressinc.com>]*

KEYWORDS. Gender variant children, transgendered children, social work practice with children

INTRODUCTION

Ma Vie en Rose (*My Life in Pink*) (Berliner, 1997) is a story about the innocence of childhood as told through the experiences of a seven

Gerald P. Mallon, DSW, is Assistant Professor, Hunter College School of Social Work, New York City, NY.

[Haworth co-indexing entry note]: "Practice with Transgendered Children." Mallon, Gerald P. Co-published simultaneously in *Journal of Gay & Lesbian Social Services* (Harrington Park Press, an imprint of The Haworth Press, Inc.) Vol. 10, No. 3/4, 1999, pp. 49-64; and: *Social Services with Transgendered Youth* (ed: Gerald P. Mallon) Harrington Park Press, an imprint of The Haworth Press, Inc., 1999, pp. 49-64. Single or multiple copies of this article are available for a fee from The Haworth Document Delivery Service [1-800-342-9678, 9:00 a.m. - 5:00 p.m. (EST). E-mail address: getinfo@haworthpressinc.com].

year old boy, Ludovic. Ludovic desperately wants to be a girl and everything about him says that he already is one. He has it all figured out; God messed up his chromosomes, simple as that, no judgement, no morality. Ludovic is a prime example of a female brain in a male body and he is putting up a valiant struggle not to be erased as a person. It's all very honest and natural to him. He is only a small boy and is much more in tune with his needs and desires than his family is.

Ludovic is a seven-year old boy, born into a middle class, suburban family. He is very much like other children, but he is also different in one key way–Ludovic is sure that he was meant to be a little girl, not a little boy–and he waits for a miracle to "correct" this mistake. Whenever he is able he dresses in typical girl outfits, he has long hair, he is certain of his gender identity despite the fact that others are less sure. His parents, while tolerant of his gender non-conforming behaviors, are also embarrassed by his insistence that he is a girl, not a boy. His siblings, although loving toward their "brother" in their home, are fatigued by having to fight for him in school when he is teased and harassed. Even though everyone else is unsure, Ludovic muddles along, praying for the miracle that will change him into the girl he knows that he is. Everything falls apart, however, when he falls in love with a boy who happens to be the son of his Father's boss–a man who is uncomfortable in his own skin.

When Ludo's father is fired from his job, because his Boss cannot abide by Ludovic's crush on his son, Ludovic's mother increasingly blames his gender non-conforming dress and behavior for the family's estrangement from their community. The gender variant behavior that was once tolerated is now insupportable–Ludovic's hair is cut into a typical boy's style; he is forced to wear traditional boy's clothing; he is brought to therapy; he is encouraged to play sports and to be more like his brothers–all "corrective" actions designed to make him to be more like a boy–to make him "fit in" by force, if necessary.

Ostracized by his schoolmates, misunderstood by his family, and eventually run out of town by bigoted neighbors, Ludovic accepts that he cannot be the boy that his family wants him to be. In a desperate attempt to break away, Ludo tries to end his life. At this point, his family realizes that in spite of what their community thinks, Ludovic should be accepted for who he or she really is. The final lines in the film are, "Do whatever feels best. Whatever happens, you'll always be my child." "Our child" is a line that every transgendered child longs to hear from his or her parent.

Ah, if life could just be as simple as it is in the movies . . . Although the film *Ma Vie en Rose (My Life in Pink)* is a powerful story of a gender variant child who struggles to be accepted by his family, childhood is undoubtedly a very difficult period for gender variant children and their parents. There are virtually no social supports in any of our social services or educational institutions for a child who is gender variant. Parents who attempt to negotiate a fair accommodation for the gender variant child will undoubtedly meet misunderstanding, incredulity, and resistance from almost everyone they encounter. "Help that child be more like a boy, get him into sports!" and "Don't let that girl be too much of a tomboy" are among the kinder things that families and gender variant children will hear.

In such a hostile environment, it is easy to blame the child for his or her failure to adapt to traditional gender norms. Often, the gender variant child will respond with depression, anxiety, fear, anger, low self-esteem, self-mutilation and suicidal ideation. Unfortunately, these at-risk behaviors are often taken as further evidence that something is wrong with the child.

Rather than putting the focus on the systems that will not allow the gender variant child to develop in his or her own natural way, "treatment" usually focuses on the child's "maladaptive" gender identity and attempts are frequently focused on "corrective" actions.

Utilizing an ecological framework (Germain, 1973, 1978, 1981), and based on the existing literature and the available research, my own twenty-four years of clinical practice with children, youth, and families, this paper examines gender variant childhood development from a holistic viewpoint where children and environments are understood as a unit, in the context of their relationship to one another (Germain, 1991, p. 16). As such, it is my goal to examine the primary reciprocal exchanges and transactions that transgendered children face as they confront the unique person:environmental tasks involved in being a gender variant child in a society that assumes all of its members are gender typical. The focus of this chapter is limited to a discussion regarding the recognition of gender identity; an examination of the adaptation process through which gender variant children deal with the stress of an environment where there is not a "goodness of fit"; and a discussion of the overall developmental tasks of a transgendered childhood. Recommendations for social work practice with gender variant children are presented in the conclusion of the paper.

Gender Identity Development in Children

Although it is a commonly-accepted fact that gender identity develops in children by the age of three, when most identify themselves as either boys or girls (Green, 1971, 1974; Meyer-Bahlburg, 1985; Money, 1973; Kohlberg, 1966; Stoller, 1965, 1968) American society steadfastly refuses to believe that children are beings with a sexuality. Because it is popularly assumed that there is a "natural" relationship between sex and gender, children who question their birth assignment are pathologized and labeled "gender dysphoric." Children who deviate from the socially-prescribed norms for boy or girl children are quickly pushed back into line by parental figures. Behaviors, mannerisms, and play which appear to be gender non-conforming to a parent, may feel normal to the child. Although gender non-conforming behavior alone does not constitute a transgendered child, Western society continues to reward parents who socialize their children to these gender-bound roles. The male child who sits with his legs crossed, the girl child who plays baseball "like a boy," the boy child who carries his books "like a girl," the girl who states that she feels uncomfortable in a dress, are examples of children who express gender variant mannerism and behavior that are natural for them.

Like the child Ludovic in *Ma Vie en Rose* who just behaved in a manner that came naturally to him, he was always surprised when others saw his gender variant behavior as "bad." The gender variant child might wonder what was so "bad" about his or her behavior that upset the parental figure. But, since most children desire to please parental figures, it is no wonder that many gender variant children go to great extremes to make adaptations to their "gender non-conforming" behaviors once they are pointed out. Other children, those who cannot change, or who refuse to change, are treated and judged much more harshly by a society that insists on adherence to strict gender norms. Children who are forced to comply with social stereotypes may develop behavioral problems, which may lead to depression and other serious mental health issues, caused not by their gender variant nature, but by society's non-acceptance of them. As Israel and Tarver (1997, p. 139) point out, it is ironic that in preventing children from exploring their gender identity, these children frequently become examples of the very stereotype the parent had hoped to prevent: a gender-conflicted adult.

Incidence of Gender Variant Children

The term "Gender Identity Disorder" first appeared in the American Psychiatric Association's DSM-III in 1980. GID is described as an "incongruence between assigned sex (i.e., the sex that is recorded on the birth certificate) and gender identity." DSM-III went on to describe a broad range of gender variant behaviors that may be observed in individuals, and insisted that "in the vast majority of cases the onset of the disorder can be traced back to childhood." GID is considered a disorder even though "some of these children, particularly girls, show no other signs of psychopathology" (American Psychiatric Association, 1980).

The introduction of GID in Children into the DSM came as the result of a United States Government-funded experiment on gender variant boys that took place in the 1970s. These studies found that very few "feminine" boys went on to become transsexuals, but that a high percentage of them (one half to two thirds) became homosexual (Burke, 1996). GID was added to the DSM-III in 1980 following the removal of homosexuality as an illness from that volume (Bern, 1993). Treatment, which was justified in the name of preventing transsexualism, focuses instead on modifying gender variant behavior and may all too easily be used to "treat" future homosexuality.

Children are particularly vulnerable to suffering medical injustices in the name of treating gender identity disorder. As legal minors, children have no legal standing to make an informed choice to refuse "treatment." The criteria for a diagnosis of gender identity disorder in children are broad, taking into account all cross-gender behavior. In boys, GID is manifest by a marked preoccupation with traditionally feminine activities: playing house, drawing pictures of beautiful girls and princesses, playing with dolls such as Barbie, playing dress-up, and having girls as playmates. Girls diagnosed with GID display intense negative reactions to parental attempts to have them wear dresses or other feminine attire.

Given the level of medical, cultural, and social misunderstanding that gender variant children will endure it is not surprising that many will develop social isolation, depression, and self-esteem problems. Children who are diagnosed with GID are often treated with brutal

aversion therapies intended to adjust or "correct" their gender orientation (Burke, 1996; Scholinsky, 1997).

Boys and girls diagnosed with gender identity disorder, as described by
Zucker and Bradley (1995, Chapter 2), display an array of sex-typed
behavior signaling a strong psychological identification with the opposite
gender. These behaviors include: (1) identity statement, (2) dress-up play,
(3) toy play, (4) role play, (5) peer relations, (6) motoric and speech
characteristics, (7) statements about sexual anatomy, and (8) involvement
in rough-and-tumble play. There are also signs of distress and discomfort
about one's status as male or female. These behaviors, note Zucker and
Bradley (1995), occur in concert, not in isolation.

The Case of Hector

Hector is a seven-year-old Latino boy of average intelligence who
was referred by his counselor at an after-school program. Hector lived
with his parents, who had a middle-class socio-economic background,
and his younger brother. His parents had noted cross-gender behavior
since the age of two. He presents as a small stature, slightly-built child,
with longish dark hair.

Hector preferred girls as playmates and since the age of two enjoyed cross-dressing both at home and in school. He had stereotypical
girl toy preferences, including a purse, a Barbie doll, and jewelry. He
sometimes spoke in a high-pitched voice, and spoke of wanting to
marry a boy when he grew up. Hector avoided rough play and sometimes verbally stated that he wished that he did not have a penis
because he was a girl, not a boy, and girls did not have penises.

The Case of Liza

Liza is a six-year-old girl with a 105 I.Q. who was referred at her
mother's request. Her parents are of working class socio-economic
background. Liza's father was concerned about his daughter's gender
non-conforming behavior. Her mother was less concerned, but agreed
to have her evaluated to appease her husband.

Liza wore jeans and a white tee shirt with a hooded sweatshirt
which she hid behind for the first half of the interview. When she
became more comfortable, she allowed the hood to fall and it was
noted that her hair was short and styled in a fashion that is more

characteristic of a boy's haircut. She noted that people frequently mistook her for a boy, particularly if she was in the women's rest room.

At age three, Liza's mother reported that she steadfastly refused to wear a dress, and in fact would throw a temper tantrum when asked to do so. Liza reported that she hated dresses and preferred to be free to dress as she pleased.

Liza preferred boys as play partners, engaged in baseball, hockey and other outdoor sports, and spoke openly about wishing that she were a boy, not a girl. Liza spoke openly about having "the operation" to become a boy when she was older. When asked to draw a picture of herself, she drew a boy with bulging muscles, which she indicated looked like her hero, "Goldberg," the World Championship Wrestling (W.C.W.) champ.

Although some may view the conditions of Liza and Hector through a lens of pathology, others who approach practice from a trans-affirming perspective may ask, Why can't Liza construct her identity to be male as she sees it, and how can it be so terrible if Hector envisions himself as a girl? The larger question is: Why are gender variant children so disturbing to people, especially to parents?

Is Gender Identity Disorder in Childhood Really a Disorder?

From a strictly diagnostic perspective, if the child meets the criteria as established for Gender Identity Disorder in Childhood in DSM-IV (American Psychiatric Association, 1994, p. 537-538), then it is not difficult to make a diagnosis. However, it should also be considered, based on the sketchy history of this diagnostic category, that one must also consider whether or not gender identity disorder is really a disorder. One of the criteria for a disorder is whether or not the persons diagnosed are distressed by their condition. Are gender variant children distressed by their condition, and if so, what is the source of their distress? Do they become distressed when they are told that they cannot be what they are sure they are? Are they distressed because of the social ostracism they must endure?

In my own clinical experiences with transgendered children, I have seen children who have been more harmed than helped by clinicians that insist on "correcting" gender variant children by attempting to make them more gender conforming. One only need to read the superb memoir of Daphne Scholinski (1987) or the powerful work of Feinberg (1993) to see that these attempts miserably fail. With true trans-gendered children (and yes, there are some children for whom this is not a genuine gender identity issue but a phase of development), no treatment program, no residential program, no group therapy, no aversion treatment plan could change who they are.

I have more often than not, seen parents who are greatly distressed by their gender variant child. Even mild, typical gender non-conformity sends terror into the hearts of most parents. One student of mine who was a mother panicked when her six-year-old son asked for an "Easy-Bake Oven." What's so scary I asked? "It's a girl toy, what do you think I should do?" "Buy the oven," I said, "if you can afford it, and then in a couple of weeks your child will either enjoy it as his favorite toy, or cast it aside when the next new toy arrives."

But such simplistic advice provides no solace for other parents. They are embarrassed, guilty, ashamed, and fearful that somehow their parenting was to blame for what went wrong, as the following case illustrates:

> Mark was an 8-year-old American-born Trinadadian child referred by his great-grandmother's Medicaid social worker. Mark was of average intelligence, his family background was working class socio-economically, and they lived in a housing project in Brooklyn.
>
> On the day of the interview, Mark arrived for the interview dressed in girl's clothing, accompanied by his great-grandmother. There was an obvious warm and affectionate relationship that existed between the two, although there were also some negative feelings due to Mark's insistence that he was a girl. Mark's great-grandmother explained that it was causing her great distress that Mark was insisting that he was a girl. She feared losing her standing in the community because neighbors began to ask her what she had done to make the child "that way." She was embarrassed by Mark's cross-dressing, by his insistence on being called by his preferred name, "Monique" and by other gender non-conforming mannerisms and behaviors. Mark simply said, "I can't be what I am not, and I am not a boy." Mark's great-grandmother said to the interviewer, "Mister, I have one question for you. Can you change him back?" When I replied, "No," she retorted, "Then you can keep him." As she got up to leave, I

stopped her and explained that she could not leave her great-grandson with me. When we explored out-of-home placement options, the prospects were quite dismal as transgendered children are not easily accepted in child welfare agencies. After some discussion she agreed that he could stay at home with her, but we settled on a treatment plan that included some compromises for both her and her grandson. It was not an ideal plan, but it was a better scheme than out-of-home placement.

Transgendered Children and Their Families

Although some transgendered children are healthy and resilient, many gender variant children are at great risk within their family system and within institutional structures. Gender variant children, because they are told that they do not fit in, are in a constant search for an affirming environment, where they can be themselves. In the search for this situation, many transgendered youth are at risk for depression, anxiety, self-abuse, substance abuse, suicide, and family violence.

Parents seeking to find answers may seek to have their transgendered child "cured" through punishment, physical violence, or endless mental health assessments. Transgendered children may be locked in their rooms, and denied opportunities to socialize. Transgendered children, as in the story of Ludovic, are viewed as the problem in the family. Such classification leads them to be scapegoated by the family, becoming the blame for everything that goes wrong.

Some transgendered children are shipped away to behavioral camps, psychiatric hospitals, or Residential Treatment Facilities, where rigidly enforced gender conformity further represses their needs and does more harm than good. In my 24 years of experience in child welfare, I have rarely come across a mental health professional or social worker, who is knowledgeable and proficient about working with a transgendered child in an affirming manner. Most do not understand the condition, and very few have ever had training to prepare them for competent practice with transgendered children. At present, very few gender-specialized services exist in mental health and child welfare systems across the country. Green Chimneys in New York and GLASS in Los Angeles are two exceptions. Regrettably, most schools of social work are not preparing practitioners to respond to the needs of this population.

Israel and Tarver (1997, pp. 134-135) observe, "as there are no treatment models for curing transgendered feelings, needs and behaviors, one is left to wonder what types of treatment transgendered children endure at the hands of parents and professionals. Such treatment approaches are little more than abuse, professional victimization, and profiteering under the guise of support for a parent's goals."

Many parents are initially surprised when they hear a trans-affirming professional state that compromise is the best approach to supporting children who have strong transgender feelings and need. After all, don't parents always know what is best for their children? Based on the high incidence of familial abuse (both verbal and physical) which I have witnessed, in the case of transgendered children, I would have to answer "No." Parents do not have training or preparation for dealing with a transgendered child. Recommendations for parents are presented in the conclusion of this paper.

Transgendered Children in Educational Settings

Schools unfortunately are among the least affirming environments of all for gender variant children. Children who are perceived as gender variant are targeted by school officials, as children to be closely monitored.

Gender variant boys are mercilessly teased for not being rough-and-tumble, they are frequently assumed to be gay by those adults who are ill-informed, and some are moved toward what I term–"the sports corrective." They are pushed into organized sports teams as though participation in such activities will correct their gender non-conformity.

Gender variant girls are also verbally harassed, but for being too much like a boy and not enough like a girl. Although other girls seldom nowadays wear dresses, gender variant girls are always confronted by both peers and adults who try to enroll them in what I term "the etiquette corrective." "Turn them tomboys into ladies and everything will be all right." It seldom, if ever, works for them. It only adds to the pain and the self-blame, as this vignette from Scholinski (1997) illustrates:

> Pinning me to the ground, the girls at school forced red lipstick onto my mouth . . . the social worker with the pointy high heels said I was wrecking the family and that if I kept things up the way they were going, with my bad behavior getting all of the

attention, my parents were going to lose my sister too. I knew I was bad, I wasn't crazy though. (p. 6)

Confusing Gender Variant Children with Gay or Lesbian Children

Gender variant children have frequently been confused with children who are gay or lesbian. In fact, many of the same diagnostic criteria that are used to justify a diagnosis of gender identity disorder, are also "cues" to a gay or lesbian identity. Many gay boys play with girls, enjoy girl toys, have effeminate mannerisms, and avoid rough-and-tumble play. Many young lesbians enjoy playing with the boys, play sports and games associated with boys, possess mannerisms and speech associated with boys, and dress in typical boy clothing. The biggest difference is that gay boys and lesbian girls generally do not express a dissatisfaction with their gender, that is, their maleness or femaleness. There are some cases, when children with limited information about their emerging gay or lesbian identity, may speak about *wishing* that they were a boy or a girl, but seldom do they state that they *are* a boy or a girl. The following case illustration represents an example of this misperception.

David is a 10-year-old Latino child who was referred to me because his therapist felt inadequate in treating what he was describing as a transgendered child. David lives with his mother, her second husband, a younger sister, and an older brother in a two-bedroom, middle income housing project in New York City. An MSW therapist at a community mental health clinic sees both David and his mother. David is bright, very verbal and precocious. The interview, which consisted of David, his therapist, his Mother and me, began with a series of questions initiated by David. Who was I? Was I a doctor? Why was I interested in seeing him? I answered directly and honestly and then proceeded with my own questions. First, given that he was a bright child, what were his career ambitions? He asked if he could draw his answer, and on his own pad of paper, which he had with him, he drew a naked boy. When I asked what it represented, he informed me that he wanted to be the first nude male dancer. He suggested that if he was a naked dancer, then boys would like him. He then went on to explain that first he would need "the operation" because the only way he could get boys to like him was if he was a girl.

He asked if he could share a secret with me, and when I agreed, he identified himself, on another piece of paper, as GAY. He also inquired as to whether or not I was gay, and then whether or not his therapist was gay. We all answered the question posed to us. He was also clear, when probed, that he did not see himself as a girl, but felt that in order to get boys to like him, he needed to become a girl and for that he would have to have "the operation."

Based on this interview, this did not seem to me to be a child who was transgendered, but a child who was gay and in need of some accurate information about his sexual identity development. I also sensed that there might be some issues of sexual abuse occurring in the household. When I inquired about his older brother and his step-father, he responded with answers which required further exploration. Since that was not the purpose of the interview, I passed that insight along to the child's therapist.

In this case, it was fairly clear that David was not transgendered as he seemed comfortable in his gender identity, but self-identified as gay in his sexual identity. In other instances, it may not always be so clear. Just as it is important that transgendered children are not mislabeled as gay or lesbian, although they frequently self-label as such prior to coming to a full understanding of their transgendered nature, it is also important that gay and lesbian children are not mislabeled as transgendered. Coming to understand the childhood experiences of transgendered persons is a complex phenomenon that requires training and supervision from a trained and skilled trans-affirming social worker. Practitioners who listen carefully to the narratives of children, and who do not permit their own negative judgements about transgendered persons to misguide them, are the most effective. The following section provides further recommendations for practice with transgendered children and their parents.

IMPLICATIONS FOR PRACTICE

Social workers who are unfamiliar with transgendered children's issues need guidance about how to proceed. The recommendations listed below provide a foundation framework for practitioners interested in enhancing their practice with transgendered children and their parents.

1. Social workers should first begin by educating themselves about transgendered children. Practitioners should not wait until they have a transgendered child in their office to seek out information. Books, especially those written by transgendered persons, several of which have been identified here in this paper and in others in this collection, are extremely useful ways of gathering information about transgendered persons. Films, which portray transgendered persons through a non-pathological lens, most specifically *Ma Vie en Rose* which is available in video stores, can be extremely informative and enlightening. Professional articles, when they can be found, are also helpful. The Internet provides a rich array of resources and information for all that have access to a computer and a modem. As bibliotherapy has been proven to be useful with clients, many of these materials, print, video, and virtual, can also be shared with clients to increase their information and knowledge.

2. Social workers should assist parents in resisting electro-shock, reparative, or aversion-type treatments outright. These are unethical practices and do not help the child.

3. Treatments for depression and associated conditions should not attempt to enforce gender stereotypical behavior and should focus on practice from a trans-affirming perspective.

4. Social workers should assist parents in developing mutually acceptable compromise strategies which can include asking the gender variant child to dress in original gender clothing for formal events such as weddings, but permitting the child to dress androgynously for school and for peer activities. Children who insist on using opposite gendered names can be encouraged to adopt an androgynous name until they are old enough to be certain that they want to change their name permanently.

5. Parents and children must work with practitioners to keep communication open. All children, despite gender issues, need love, acceptance, and compassion from their families. It is one of the things they fear losing the most. Children need to be reminded that their parents' love for them is unconditional.

6. Practitioners need to be able to identify resources for trans-children and families in the community, or be willing to take the risk necessary to create them.
7. Transgendered children should be assisted with developing strategies for dealing with societal stigmatization, name-calling, and discrimination.
8. In completing an assessment of a transgendered child, the social worker should be familiar with the criteria in DSM-IV for gender identity disorder, be comfortable with discerning the differences between a gay, lesbian, bisexual, or questioning child and a transgendered child, and utilize a modified version of Israel and Tarvers' (1997, pp. 151-163) Gender Identity Profile.
9. The decision-making process for any gender procedure must include consideration of the critical factors of age, maturity, and physical development. Hormone administration and genital reassignment surgery is obviously not advised during childhood.
10. Practitioners should be aware that transgendered children are part of every culture, race, religion, and experience. Transgendered children of color and their families face compounded stressors resulting from transgenderphobia and racism and may need additional emotional and social support, as well as legal redress of discrimination.
11. Practitioners should be aware that individual, self-help, family, and group treatment approaches are all appropriate for intervening with a transgendered child and his or her family.
12. Practitioners must be aware of the possibility that violence both within and outside of the child's family may be directed toward the transgendered child. Sexual violence, including rape, is also prevalent and should be closely monitored by the practitioner.
13. Practitioners must be ready to respond to, and to reach out to siblings, grandparents, and other relatives of the transgendered child to provide education, information and support.
14. Practitioners should help parents understand that gender variant children's behaviors and mannerisms are natural to them.
15. Practitioners should help parents to develop a strategy for addressing the questions that neighbors and members of the community may have about their transgendered child.
16. Schools, social service, child welfare systems, mental health systems, religious institutions are all likely to encounter gender-

variant youth. These organizations and the individuals who work within them need to identify consultants to act as trans-affirming professional guides, and provide in-service training to assist them with the process of becoming trans-affirming systems. These systems must set about *trans*-forming their organizational cultures to include sensitive and welcoming services for all children, youth, and families. Child welfare systems, which are residential in nature, and may have unique issues, will need specialized training to care for transgendered children and their families.

17. Gay, lesbian, bisexual, and questioning youth providers must also work to respond to the unique needs of transgendered children. Most GLBQ organizations solely meet the needs of teens and young adults; services for younger youth should also be explored.

18. Practitioners must accept the reality that not everyone can provide validation for a transgendered child. Some will simply not be able to understand the turmoil and pain transgendered children experience.

CONCLUSIONS

I cannot think of a better way to conclude this paper than to pay homage to the powerful words of Leslie Feinberg, transgendered activist, who knew firsthand the pain that accompanies the life of a transgendered child.

> I didn't want to be different. I longed to be everything grownups wanted, so they would love me. I followed their rules, tried my best to please. But there was something about me that made them knit their eyebrows and frown. No one ever offered me a name for what was wrong with me. That's what made me afraid it was really bad. I only came to recognize its melody through its constant refrain: "Is it a boy or a girl?"

> "I'm sick of people asking me if she's a boy or a girl," I overheard my mother complain to my father. "Everywhere I take her, people ask me."

I was ten years old. I was no longer a little kid and I didn't have a sliver of cuteness to hide behind. The world's patience with me was fraying, and it panicked me. When I was really small I thought I would do anything to change whatever was wrong with me. Now I didn't want to change, I just wanted people to stop being mad at me all the time. (Feinberg, 1993, p. 13, 19)

REFERENCES

American Psychiatric Association. (1980). *Diagnostic and statistical manual of mental disorders* (3rd ed.). Washington, DC: Author.
American Psychiatric Association. (1994). *Diagnostic and statistical manual of mental disorders* (4th ed.). Washington, DC: Author.
Berliner, A. (1997). *Ma Vie en Rose*. Los Angeles: SONY Classics.
Bern, S. L. (1993). *The lenses of gender*. New Haven: Yale University Press.
Burke, P. (1996). *Gender shock: Exploding the myths of male and female*. NY: Bantam Books.
Feinberg, L. (1993). *Stone butch blues*. Ithaca, NY: Firebrand Books.
Germain, C. B. (1973). The ecological perspective in casework practice. *Social Casework: The Journal of Contemporary Social Work, 54*, 323-330.
Germain, C. B. (1978). General-systems theory and ego psychology: An ecological perspective. *Social Service Review*, 535-550.
Germain, C. B. (1981). The ecological approach to people-environment transactions. *Social Casework: The Journal of Contemporary Social Work, 62*, 323-331.
Germain, C. B. (1991). *Human behavior and the social environment*. New York: Columbia University Press.
Green, R. (1971). Diagnosis and treatment of gender identity disorders during childhood. *Archives of Sexual Behavior, 1*, 167-174.
Green, R. (1974). *Sexual identity conflict in children and adults*. New York: Basic Books.
Israel, G., & Tarver, D. (1997). *Transgender Care: Recommended Guidelines, Practical Information and Personal Accounts*. Philadelphia: Temple University Press.
Kohlberg, L. (1966). A cognitive-developmental analysis of children's sex-role concepts and attitudes. In E.E. Maccoby (Ed.), *The development of sex differences* (pp. 82-173). Stanford, CA: Stanford University Press.
Meyer-Bahlberg, H.F.L. (1985). Gender identity disorder of childhood: Introduction. *Journal of the American Academy of Child Psychiatry, 24*, 681-683.
Money, J. (1973). Gender role, gender identity, core gender identity: Usage and definition of terms. *Journal of the American Academy of Psychoanalysis, 1*, 397-403.
Scholinski, D. (1997). *The last time I wore a dress*. New York: Riverhead Books.
Stoller, R.J. (1965). The sense of maleness. *Psychoanalytic Quarterly, 34*, 207-218.
Stoller, R.J. (1968). The sense of femaleness. *Psychoanalytic Quarterly, 37*, 42-55.
Zucker, K.J., & Bradley, S.J. (1995). *Gender identity disorder in children and psychosexual problems in children and adolescents*. New York: Guilford Press.

Practice with Female-to-Male Transgendered Youth

Sophia Pazos

SUMMARY. This paper examines the multiple experiences of female-to-male transgendered identified adolescents also known as FTMs. The information utilized in this paper is based on the available literature on FTMs and the result of over two years of listening to the narratives of FTM transgendered adolescents with whom I have worked and from professional counseling experiences with several FTMs ranging in age from their mid to late teens to their early forties. The paper also focuses on current theories, offers a strengths-based approach to practice, and concludes with implications for practice with FTM clients. *[Article copies available for a fee from The Haworth Document Delivery Service: 1-800-342-9678. E-mail address: getinfo@haworthpressinc.com <Website: http://www.haworthpressinc.com>]*

KEYWORDS. FTM, transgendered female-to-male youth, social work practice with adolescents

INTRODUCTION

Adolescence is a period of development focused on discovering one's role and identity in the world. It is a time of exploration, self-discovery and testing new independence. Such challenges and changes spark anxiety and stress for all adolescents especially if they cannot

---

Sophia Pazos is a social worker at the Jewish Board of Children and Family Services AIDS Family Volunteer Program in Brooklyn, New York.

[Haworth co-indexing entry note]: "Practice with Female-to-Male Transgendered Youth." Pazos, Sophia. Co-published simultaneously in *Journal of Gay & Lesbian Social Services* (Harrington Park Press, an imprint of The Haworth Press, Inc.) Vol. 10, No. 3/4, 1999, pp. 65-82; and: *Social Services with Transgendered Youth* (ed: Gerald P. Mallon) Harrington Park Press, an imprint of The Haworth Press, Inc., 1999, pp. 65-82. Single or multiple copies of this article are available for a fee from The Haworth Document Delivery Service [1-800-342-9678, 9:00 a.m. - 5:00 p.m. (EST). E-mail address: getinfo@haworthpressinc.com].

conform to the social norms expected from their peer group, family, and/or community. Adolescents who are gay, lesbian, bisexual, and transgender feel their difference more deeply. One person that I interviewed described it as "living alone with a chasm between me and the rest of the world."

While there is increasingly ample literature that documents the challenges of gay and lesbian adolescents, there are very few works about adolescents of transgender experience (Israel & Tarver, 1997). Many helping professionals erroneously perceive gender difference (termed by most as gender dysphoria) as an indicator of homosexuality or inherently pathology. Some social workers and mental health practitioners act upon these feelings treating transgendered youth as though they are dysfunctional. The literature which does exist also concentrates on the intrapsychic characteristics of transgenderism ignoring how the various systems in the environment contribute to the person's overall mental health. Finally, the preponderance of literature is based on research with male-to-female transsexuals, which is a significant population to be studied, but a population with a very different experience.

This paper examines the multiple experiences of female-to-male transgendered identified adolescents also known as FTMs. The information utilized in this paper is based on the available literature on FTMs and the result of over two years of listening to the narratives of FTM transgendered adolescents with whom I have worked and from professional counseling experiences with several FTMs ranging in age from their mid to late teens to their early forties. For the most part, individuals who are active in the transgender community are persons who have been able to afford treatment and surgery and keep in contact via the Internet. As such, the majority of the individuals I worked with are white, and socio-economically from middle and upper class backgrounds. Two individuals with whom I worked were African Americans; one was Native American. Literature reflecting the experiences of transgender people of color and transgender individuals living in poverty and isolation from a larger community is utterly lacking.

Gender History and Theory

It is easy to presume that gender is always seen from two absolute perspectives, male and female, blue and pink. Feinberg (1993) documents several instances in the history of Western Europe where gender variance existed. Joan of Arc, Amelia Earhart, and "Rebecca's Daughters" (cross-dressing Welsh resistance fighters) are all examples of women who defied the traditional female assigned roles that society prescribed for them. Although their communities initially may have treated these women with scorn, they were ultimately esteemed by the people in the communities where they lived. Gender diversity also had its place in non-Western societies. Various Native American cultures performed rituals in which children chose what gender roles they preferred. These "not-men" and "not-women" were often revered and given important status (Brown, 1997; Jacobs, Thomas & Lang, 1997).

Society's aversion to gender ambiguity is another area which has not been borne out by science (Fausto-Sterling, 1993). In reality, there are naturally occurring genetic mutations that result in gender ambiguity. Medical professionals argue that there are several criteria for determining sex: secondary sex characteristics, genetic makeup, hormone levels, and genitalia. Yet most people, even newborn infants, are assigned a gender according to the observation of external genitalia.

Gender theory is evolving rapidly in different fields of academic discourse. Bornstein (1994) for example argues that gender is essentially a binary class system in which one class will always try to oppress the other. Bornstein's perspective further posits that there will never be any true freedom and equality until all gender is done away with and relegated to nothing more than conscious choice. Others (Garber, 1992; Paglia, 1991; Steiner, 1981) discuss gender in terms of feminism, politics, and spirituality. Social work, unfortunately, has been slow to join in this debate.

Trends Experienced by FTMs During Childhood

As early as five years of age, many FTMs already reported that they had an awareness that something was "different" about them (Scholinski, 1997). Many reported feelings of shock when they realized their bodies were different from those of biological males, as this young person reported:

> The first time I saw my brother naked, I couldn't understand how I felt so much like him but he had totally different body parts.

As a means of coping with the daily stress of living in a hostile environment, many FTMs reported engaging in magical thinking and daydreaming about being a boy. Such adaptive strategies continued well into their pre-teen years. Some even verbalized their wishes to others:

> When I was little, I would go whine to my mother; I'm tired of being a girl; can I be a boy now?

In attempting to "make the change" some FTMs tried to adopt male external genitalia, creating penises for themselves with toys or socks and attempting to urinate standing up. Many females who experienced their lives as male, reported that they refused to wear shirts or bathing suits during the summer, preferring to wear bathing trunks like boys. Nearly all of the FTMs I spoke with reported that they enjoyed traditionally male-oriented activities such as baseball, soccer, and basketball as children. Most recalled that they preferred pants over skirts, wanted their hair cut short and wanted to socialize with boys as friends. When these children played with girls, many preferred to be the husband in a game of house or they were assigned by the other children to be the husband, as if the other children tacitly understood their female friend to be male. In her brilliant memoir, entitled *The Last Time I Wore a Dress*, author Daphne Scholinski (1997, p. 30), a person of transgendered experience, corroborates this point:

> I wore Toughskin jeans with double-thick knees so I could wrestle with Jean and the neighborhood boys. My mother cut my hair short so father wouldn't brush my long-hair snarls with No More Tangles spray. I took off my shirt in summer when the heat in Illinois smothered me in the yard and I got on my bike and glided down the hill no-handed. The wind on my chest felt like freedom until three boys in the neighborhood saw me and said, Daphne, let me see your titties, which was ridiculous since my chest was as flat as theirs but they held me on the ground. My ride was ruined and I put on a shirt, but not before I punched one of them hard in the stomach and they all backed off. (Scholinski, 1997, p. 46)

In some cases, it seemed as though professionals also tacitly understood gender issues in some children, as this quote, also from Scholinski (p. 30), suggests:

They sent me to the school counselor . . . her favorite game was The Career Game. She held up cards with pictures of a policeman, a farmer, a construction worker, a secretary, a nurse, and I said which ones I'd like to be: police officer and construction worker. She looked at me with a curious face . . . she was one of the first ones who said I had a problem with my gender. I didn't know what that meant, but I found out later. I found out she thought I wanted to be a boy.

Family reaction to the "tomboyishness" of their female youth varied. Younger FTMs, raised during the seventies and eighties, reported that gender difference was for the most part, ignored or tolerated by their families. They attributed this to the fact that gender roles for men and women had changed due to the feminist movements of the sixties and seventies. One woman recalled:

I think my mom thought my "tomboy phase" was my way of empowering myself. She never tried to change the way I looked or acted. She just bought me tailored slacks for special occasions.

FTMs raised fifteen years earlier remembered daily battles with their parents demanding that they dress and act more "ladylike," as this woman remembered:

When I was six, seven years old it was still rare to see girls in pants so I had to wear a skirt every day to school. Needless to say I hated waking up in the morning, because I knew that I would have to wear a skirt.

Scholinski (1997) had a comparable memory:

When I was little my mother would dress me in a frilly dress and comb my hair back tight along my scalp. My dress was immaculate and stiff. I couldn't wait to take off my dress and be myself again. When I wore a dress I'd be flooded with remarks—"Oooh, you look so pretty today"—which were meant to inspire me but it didn't. I wasn't interested with being pretty. I wanted to be free to run. I hated that I couldn't wear what I wanted and be left alone about it. (p. 30 & p. 59)

When families had frequent social obligations, i.e., clubs, church, or when they occupied a more elevated socio-economic status, they tended to place more emphasis on their daughter's need to act feminine. Some families attempted to persuade their "gender different" children to conform by enrolling them in "socially corrective" situations, like etiquette classes, charm school, and the Girl Scouts. One FTM remembers his disappointment at joining the Girl Scouts where instead of camping they learned how to make silver polish. Scholinski (1997, p. 97) self-defined this phenomenon as "trying to make me into a girly-girl."

In some cases, with the older group, there was verbal abuse which was clearly associated with their perceived "gender deviance."

At school, FTMs were often the target of verbal harassment by both male and female peers. The most frequent verbal assaults hurled at them included the words: "lezzie," "dyke," "freak," or "tomboy." Many FTMs responded by engaging in physical confrontations with peers or by withdrawing altogether from social activities.

> I was having trouble with friends. The boys who teased me about not wearing a shirt in the summer came after me, called out "tomboy, tomboy" and knocked my books out of my arms, so other kids stayed away from me. (Scholinski, 1997, p. 69)

Some involved themselves in solitary activities such as academics, reading, and writing. As they entered their pre-teen years, many FTMs became involved in any activity that would allow them to engage in fantasy. A large proportion of FTMs I spoke to had interests in drama, science fiction, and role playing games. A majority of FTMs in their twenties and thirties were self-described computer "geeks" and remember first immersing themselves in computers as a means of escape from reality.

Adolescence

Brown and Rownsley (1996) describe puberty for transsexuals as "nature's cruel trick." Puberty brings about the end of the fantasizing and magical thinking FTMs used to cope. As their bodies develop secondary sexual characteristics (breasts grow, hips widen and menarche begins), their world of fantasy, which permits them to envision themselves as male, crumbles. Reactions in the individuals I interviewed ranged from shock to betrayal and disgust. One individual understood the experience of change this way:

> I saw all these changes going on with my body and all I could think of was NO.

> All my praying didn't work. I hated God for a long time. Not only was I born with a female body but He had to go and give me large breasts as well.

> I didn't want to believe it was happening. I had to be forced to wear a bra and I ruined some underwear before I realized I couldn't deny my period.

Wearing men's clothes, binding breasts, and pants stuffing became even more imperative in order to feel comfortable in one's body. When these options weren't possible, FTMs used disassociation as a coping mechanism. The FTMs I have worked with went "through the motions of living," detaching emotionally from their bodies. Others acted out against their bodies on a more subconscious level by developing eating disorders or becoming accident-prone. In more extreme cases, FTMs have self-mutilated, usually slashing or pounding on their chest until it was bruised (Brown & Rownsley, 1996).

FTMs currently in their twenties and thirties did not have the language to express the emotions they felt. Transsexuality was not part of everyday conversation. Except for some references to male to female cross dressers, FTMs did not see themselves represented–they were an invisible and marginalized population. The refusal to allow this invisibility to continue into the next generation has been the primary motivation for all of them to take on some sort of public role to prevent other gender different teens from suffering the same traumas.

There is a lower incidence of negative body images among the younger FTMs who I spoke with. Many credited this to their early awareness of transgenderism and FTM transsexuality, in some cases augmented by the Internet, which they felt helped create a psychological and physical support system. The Internet has opened the closet door for transgendered persons. The ability to gather information about one's identity, to communicate with others who share your experience, and at the same time to remain anonymous, has liberated thousands from the gloom of the closet. This young person's recollection confirmed this:

> I saw S.'s web page with his diary about his transition and everything made sense. Through S. I am now connected with other FTMs my age. It's made looking in the mirror a little less difficult.

Social support was identified as a huge factor in how FTMs survived in the most hostile system affecting their lives: the high school.

FTMs and High School

Although many FTMs were the target for verbal taunts by their peers, many also found their niche in the social hierarchy of high school. Some excelled in academics or athletics. Others continued with their interests in drama, role playing, and computers. Being involved in various activities was a way of keeping busy and not thinking about their inner turmoil (Brown & Rownsley, 1996). A positive result of these prominent social activities was being able to identify one or two close friends who accepted their "quirky" behaviors. One young man suggested that the presence of these significant friendships made a difference in how FTMs functioned emotionally:

> I made friends with some of the guys from a club who related to me as a guy, which was a lifesaver for me.

> My best friend was a girl from the soccer team who didn't seem to care that I wasn't interested in girl things and liked that I acted like a brother.

Although these social friendships were rewarding, dating was usually a frustrating experience. Dating patterns with FTMs usually fell into two extreme categories.

- FTMs who identified as heterosexual saw teenage boys as friends and were shocked and disappointed when male friends had a romantic interest in them, but, many believed that dating girls was not an option. Gender and sexual orientation once again played a very complex role in this process. In a female-appearing body, FTMs would be perceived as lesbian, when in their minds they were dating the opposite sex. FTMs who identified as gay wanted to date boys but did not want to relate to them sexually in a female body. Stuck in this catch-22, many FTMs chose not to date either gender or dated very rarely.
- FTMs who became involved in several sexual and romantic encounters as a means of proving that they are normal. By dating several boys, rumors of being lesbian would usually subside.

Some FTMs also dated boys as a way of living vicariously through their boyfriends, as this young man recalled:

> I loved dating guys because then I had an excuse to go to the department store and buy men's clothes and colognes "for my boyfriend."

Some FTMs felt that they were in fact lesbians. In a society that equates gender difference with homosexuality, this was a natural assumption. Depending on their own feelings about gays and lesbians this either brought comfort to some or added to their stress. Depending on where they lived and the resources which were or were not available for gay and lesbian youth, some FTMs came out and lived as lesbians first before identifying as transgendered later. This is a very important phenomenon for social workers to understand.

On the whole, high school evoked painful memories for most of the young people that I interviewed. Undressing in locker rooms and using bathrooms represented moments of extreme anxiety. Scholinski (1997) has vivid narratives about bathroom use:

> "This is the line for the women's room." "I know." I looked at her as if she was the fool, but inside I was sweating. She reminded me again. "I am a woman." I hated saying that: I have never quite fit in that box. She said, "You don't look like a woman. You don't sound like a woman." What was I supposed to do with that? I was like, "What do you want to see my i.d.?" I pulled my i.d. out of my wallet and showed her. I knew I didn't have to do it, but I thought it would end it. I avoid public bathrooms. I'll never be a girly-girl. (p. 194)

Despite having friends, some FTMs still felt they were living lives of deception and invested a great deal of energy into trying to conform to the social norms assigned to their biological gender. Such attempts at finding transactional fits which are positive and nurturing were an emotionally exhausting process. This, combined with the guilt and shame for being perceived as a freak, anger at not being able to be who they are, as well as the normal amount of angst associated with adolescent development, and it is not surprising that many FTMs suffer from extremely low self-esteem.

Without friends or support, many FTMs fell into deep depression. Feelings of despair and isolation often led to self-medication with drugs, alcohol, and other chemical substances. Although there are no statistics that speak to issues of drug abuse among FTMs, over half of the individuals I interviewed are currently in recovery programs. All of those interviewed traced part of their addiction to their emotions regarding their gender difference. Others reported that they had contemplated or attempted suicide. The comments of this young man confirm that there may be more transgendered youth that hold these feelings:

> Since I first came out in 1995, I've lost two friends and had at least five others try suicide. There are probably lots more than the research shows since FTMs and other transgender teens are still invisible.

FTMs and the Family

Families of FTMs that I interviewed may not have been accepting of their gender variant child, but at the very least they were described as tolerant of a "tomboy girl." When the tomboy phase lasted longer than anticipated, most reported that their family's reaction changed. In these cases, parents exerted more pressure on their teens to conform to societally prescribed gender roles. These efforts, while often well intentioned, were misguided. They are reflected in this quotation:

> I wanted my child to be accepted by the high school. I had dreams of homecoming queen, college, and marriage. To see my daughter act so masculine and so angry . . . I thought I was doing the right thing to force her to act like a lady.

Devor (1997) interviewed several FTMs on a variety of topics including their relationships with their families during adolescence. In her work, Devor (1997) found that FTMs had close relationships with female relatives when they were able to take on protective "male head of the household" roles within the family. Relationships with female relatives were reported to be indifferent or unusually tense. Devor's (1997) work suggested that female relatives exerted more pressure on FTMs to conform to gender roles.

Devor found that relationships FTMs had with male relatives were not any better. FTMs who reported close relationships with their brothers during childhood found that adolescence caused a shift. Their brothers grew into the bodies they silently desired and gained the privileges of being male. FTMs, on the other hand, saw their bodies as having betrayed them and believed their freedom to act masculine had been curtailed. FTMs also resented how adolescence changed the way fathers treated them. FTMs found their fathers to be poor role models, partly because they could not form the father-son bond they wanted.

Increased pressure to act like a girl, coupled with an adolescent's struggle for independence, resulted in extreme tension within the family. There were frequent arguments affecting all family members. Siblings were often caught in the middle.

> I hated the fights and I loved my "sister" but it just seemed that my parents had a point. We all thought all "she" had to do was stop acting so different and everything will be all right.

When FTMs began to act out their pain, in some cases by becoming more involved with drugs and alcohol, such behavior gave families the impetus to force their children into therapy. Many times, just the gender difference was enough to push their children into therapy. If therapy failed to fix the problem, some FTM teens were psychiatrically hospitalized for treatment of gender identity disorder. The thoughts of one individual with whom I worked spoke to that horrifying experience:

> They kept me drugged at all times. They forced me to wear dresses. I'll admit I was depressed and suicidal but what did wearing dresses have to do with making me feel better? Others I knew received electric shock treatments.

When tensions reached a breaking point, some parents threw their children out of their homes. Some parents forbade their children from taking part in any family events; others were denied access to extended family, as this narrative illustrates:

> My parents sort of accept me but they rather I not attend any family functions. I'm not allowed to speak to my grandparents or other relatives. I wasn't able to see my sister graduate high school.

> In the past three years my mother has tried to have me committed, changed the locks on the doors, and tried to prevent me

from collecting my grandmother's inheritance. The other day she called saying that her divorce was all my fault.

If parents withdrew financial support, teens were left poor and homeless. Some went into foster care where they were frequent targets for abuse (Mallon, 1998). Others became transients, moving from house to house or sofa to sofa. A few joined other teens in street life, creating their own "families" using whatever means to survive, as this young person's quote suggests:

When people think about gay prostitutes they think about the gay boys and male-to-female transsexuals. But there are a lot of FTMs hustling too.

Current Theories and Treatment of Transsexuals

The Diagnostic and Statistical Manual (DSM) IV describes gender difference as Gender Identity Disorder (GID), a "persistent cross-gender identification and a persistent discomfort with his or her sex" (American Psychiatric Association, 1994). This description of transsexualism is the basis for the prevalent theory of transsexualism that views it as pathology. Viewing the client as pathological, many clinicians based their interventions on guiding the patient to accept the gender role related to their birth sex.

The presence of GID in the DSM has enabled many clinicians to use this diagnosis not only to treat transsexuals but also to apply the same therapies to gay and lesbian youth that exhibit transgender behaviors. By equating gender with sexual orientation, clinicians such as Moberly (1983) and Zucker (1990) have been able to utilize treatment approaches that are homophobic. There is a rejection of the current medical model advocated by the psychiatric profession by most in the transgender community. There is also the belief that different treatment models are essential.

Towards a Strengths Based Treatment Model

Increasingly, professionals in psychology, psychiatry, and other fields are advocating for more affirming approaches of therapeutic models for treating transsexualism. Ekins and King (1998) argue that psychiatry has viewed transsexualism from an individual perspective ignoring the societal factors that affect a person's overall mental health. Many transsexuals do not see themselves as sick but have a lower level of functioning and higher stress due to society's inability to accept gender difference. The quest for "realness" causes them additional unrest.

Schaefer, Wheeler, and Futterweit (1995) remind us that helping professionals should not make the assumption that the gender difference is the cause for all of a patient's problems. Stressing the importance of a holistic psychotherapeutic model involving education, individual and family therapy, and improving interpersonal relations rather than being hampered by "gender guilt," these authors advocate the role of a therapist as a guide to help patients understand and accept their gender difference and decide what is the best way to live with it. Their approach is clearly a departure from the traditional role of the gender therapist as a gatekeeper or judge of who is really transsexual.

Hormone Therapy

Transsexual youth have not fully benefited from these changes in approach to gender therapy. The current Standards of Care used as guidelines for treating transsexuals exclude anyone under the age of eighteen from receiving hormone therapy or sexual reassignment surgery (Israel & Tarver, 1997). Transsexual adolescents need the full support of their families to enter any kind of gender program. Helping professionals either dismiss gender difference or use interventions meant to discourage it. Even if a therapist may recommend it, very few parents grant permission.

Claudine Griggs (1998) makes several valid points in her argument that transsexual teens should be allowed to transition. Physically, hormonal therapy at adolescence would retard undesired secondary sex characteristics and enhance desired characteristics, thus eliminating the need for cosmetic surgery in the future. The psychological effect of puberty is devastating for most transsexuals. This suffering is a factor in the high incidence of depression, suicide, and substance abuse among transsexuals. Early diagnosis and treatment of transsexuals may prevent long-term psychological trauma. From a legal standpoint, an adolescent or young adult has less of a bureaucratic history (i.e., driver's license, professional credentials transcripts) that would need to change after transition. Early transition would also give transsexuals a longer period of socialization in the gender role they choose to live in. It may also help family and significant others adjust to a person's new gender identity.

Implications for Social Work Practice

Even in the best scenario, transsexual youth face great challenges. Only one state and several cities in the United States have gender identity and expression included in non-discrimination laws and ordinances. Transsexuals and transgender individuals have no legal protections, leaving them vulnerable to discrimination in housing, employment, and access to education and adequate health services. They are vulnerable to the bias of Family Court judges in cases of custody, divorce, family violence and adoption. In addition, perceived gender difference makes transgender individuals a frequent target of verbal harassment and physical attacks (National Center for Lesbian Rights, 1997).

Social workers first need to educate themselves on transgender issues, especially by familiarizing themselves with works by authors who are themselves transgender. Education on transgender issues needs to be done at all social work agencies and become part of the curriculum taught at graduate schools of social work. When counseling gender different youth and their families, a psychoeducational approach may be useful to dispel popular myths associated with transgenderism. Gender questioning youth will also need as much information as possible about support, resources and options available to them.

Counseling gender different youth from a strengths perspective involves viewing transgenderism as an integral part of the client's identity, not as a pathology. Transgender youth will often be resistant to therapy, especially if previous therapists have tried to discourage cross-gender behaviors. It is important in forming a therapeutic alliance to respect the client's wishes in being called by their preferred name (as opposed to their birth name) and using the pronoun that they prefer. If possible, clients should also have the safe space to dress in the manner in which they feel most comfortable (Israel & Tarver, 1997).

To assist families, compromises may need to be negotiated between parents and children. Such compromises may include the use of unisex names and clothing, and refraining from forcing them to dress in gender-specific clothing. Families of transsexual children need support as they will undoubtedly also "transition" along with their children. Family members will go through emotional stages similar to the grieving process: denial, anger, guilt, shame, and shock. Parents are concerned about their child's future in regards to health, employment, safety, and the chances for happy love relationships. Furthermore, family members will need to adjust to different names and pronouns. To make this shift successfully will take time (Our Trans Children, 1999).

Because of societal stressors, some transgendered youth may engage in at-risk behaviors such as substance abuse, sexual promiscuity, or prostitution and use illegally obtained hormones. Some individuals interviewed reported that their substance abuse was related to their self-hatred for being transgender. Until the person has addressed his or her low self-esteem and is ready to begin recovery, harm reduction methods, rather than complete abstinence, should be attempted. Transsexuals involved in sex work (see the paper by Klein in this collection) and sexually promiscuous behavior also need to bolster their self-esteem and will need support in finding training and educational sites that will be tolerant of gender difference. Social workers will almost assuredly need to be advocates between the client and the medical profession.

Finally, social workers need to be involved in creating policy and laws supporting the rights of transgender individuals. The International Bill of Gender Rights outlines the basic guidelines that would ensure transgender individuals full freedom and protection under the law and which may provide some clear guidance for social workers:

> The individual's right to define gender identity.
> The right to free expression of gender identity.
> The right to control and change one's own body.
> The right to competent medical and professional care.
> The right to freedom from psychiatric diagnosis and treatment.
> The right to sexual expression.
> The right to form committed loving relationships and enter marital contracts.
> The right to conceive or adopt children; the right to nurture and have custody of children and exercise of parental rights.
> (www.abamll.com/ictlep, 1998)

CONCLUSION

The Harry Benjamin International Gender Dysphoria Association recently included master's level social workers among its list of professionals qualified to be gender therapists within the Standards of Care (www.transgender.org, 1997). Because social workers are accessible to large populations, they can expect an increase of transgendered youth and their families seeking therapy and referrals. With this revision, more transsexual youth and their families will seek social workers for assistance. With increased discussion of transgender issues, agencies targeted to family, children, and youth services have seen an increase of transgender and transsexual youth seeking services. Social work has an opportunity to add a systems based and strengths based perspective to current theories on treatment and transgender youth. The social worker will have to take on roles such as therapist, advocate, and policy-maker in order to provide the best services to this growing population.

FTMs live with the double-edged sword of invisibility and passing. A female with masculine traits is either dismissed, ignored, or feared. While this may provide a mantle of safety for some time, viewing FTMs as such keeps their service needs from being fully known or addressed. Perhaps it is most appropriate for Scholinski (1997) to have the last word:

> These words [those used in DSM IV to describe gender identity disorder] are ludicrous, but not if it's you they're talking about, not if it's you they're locking up. Not ludicrous at all for the ones who continue to be diagnosed as mentally ill. A mouthy girl in cowboy boots or a boy who drapes a scarf on his head to pretend his hair is long like a princess–well, they are targets for the Dr. Madisons of the world . . . I know I could have done worse, if my father hadn't had his fat insurance policy, if I hadn't been from a middle class, white family, I could have ended up in jail instead of the psych ward. If I had been a young kid of color no one would have thought I was worth fixing. (pp. 196-197)

As more and more of these unique young people come into the open, it is a social worker's responsibility to educate, to empower, and most importantly, to listen.

REFERENCES

American Psychiatric Association. (1994). *Diagnostic and statistical manual of mental disorders (4th edition)*. Washington, DC: Author.

Bornstein, K. (1994). *Gender outlaw: On men, women, and the rest of us*. New York: Routledge.

Brown, L.B. (1997). Women and men, not-men and not-women, lesbians and gays: American Indian gender style alternatives. *Journal of Gay & Lesbian Social Services*, 6(2), 5-20

Brown, M., & Rownsley, C.A. (1996). *True Selves: Understanding transsexualism for family, friends, co-workers and helping professionals*. San Francisco: Jossey-Bass.

Devor, H. (1997). *FTM: Female to male transsexual in society*. Bloomington: Indiana University Press.

Ekins, R., & King, D. (1998). Blending genders: Contributions to the emerging field of transgender studies. In D. Denny (Ed.), *Current concepts in transgender identity*. New York: Garland Publishing, Inc.

Fausto-Sterling, A. (1993, March/April). The five sexes: Why male and female are not enough. *The Sciences*, 20-25.

Feinberg, L. (1996). *Transgender warriors: Making history from Joan of Arc to Dennis Rodman*. Boston: Beacon Press.

Garber, M. (1992). *Vested interests*. New York: Routledge, Chapman and Hall.

Griggs, C. (1998). *S/he: Changing sex and changing clothes*. Oxford: Berg.

Harry Benjamin International Gender Dysphoria Association. (n.d./1997). *The standards of care*: The hormonal and surgical sex reassignment of gender dysphoric persons. [www document]. http:/www.transgender.org/tg/ifge/archive/SOC.

Israel, G., & Tarver, D. (1997). *Transgender care: Recommended guidelines, practical information and personal accounts*. Philadelphia: Temple University Press.

Jacobs, S., Thomas, W., & Lang, S. (Eds.). (1997). *Two-spirit people: Native American gender identity, sexuality, and spirituality*. Chicago: University of Illinois Press.

Kessler, S., & McKenna, W. (1978). *Gender: An ethnomethodological approach*. New York: John Wiley and Sons

Lothstein, L. (1983). *Female-to-Male transsexualism: Historical, clinical and theoretical issues*. Boston: Routledge.

Mallon, G.P. (1998). *We don't exactly get the welcome wagon: The experiences of gay and lesbian adolescents in child welfare systems*. New York: Columbia University Press.

Moberly, E. (1983). *Psychogenesis: The early development of gender identity*. London: Routledge & Kegan Paul Ltd.

National Center for Lesbian Rights (1997). *Handbook for transgender rights*. San Francisco: Author.

Our Trans Children. (1999). A publication of the Transgender Special Outreach Network of Parents, Families and Friends of Lesbian and Gays (TSON-PFLAG). Washington, DC.

Paglia, C. (1991). *Sexual persona*. New York: Vintage Books.

Schaefer, L.C., Wheeler, C.C., & Futterweit, W. (1995). *Gender identity disorders in treatment of psychiatric disorders, Volume 2.* Washington, DC: American Psychiatric Association.

Scholinski, D. (1997). *The last time I wore a dress.* New York: Riverhead Books.

Steiner, B.W. (1981). From Sappho to Sand: Historical perspectives on cross-dressing and cross gender. *Canadian Journal of Psychiatry, 36,* 502-506.

The International Conference on Transgender Law and Employment Policy. (n.d./1998). *International Bill of Gender Rights.* [www document]. http://www.abmall.com/ictlep

Transgender Legal Issues: An overview of selected issues. (1997). San Francisco: National Center for Lesbian Rights.

Wheeler, C.C. & Schaefer, L.C. (1997). Clinical treatment of gender identity conditions. Workshop given at the Third Annual All-FTM Conference, Boston, Massachusetts.

Zucker, K. (1990). Treatment of gender identity disorders in children. In R. Blanchard & B. Steiner (Eds.), *Clinical management of gender identity disorders in children and adults* (pp. 2015-2079). Washington DC: American Psychiatric Press.

Reflections
of an Emerging Male-to-Female
Transgendered Consciousness

Wendell D. Glenn

SUMMARY. Professionals involved in social work practice with or designing approaches for working with male-to-female (MTF) transgendered youth must listen to the individual voices of these youth for the valuable information they can share with us. This paper provides the reader with the gift of a first-person account of one person's experiences as a "plainclothes transgender" person–a term he has coined to define his experiences. The paper concludes with implications for practice with both "plainclothes" and "fixed/prepared" male-to-female transgendered youth. *[Article copies available for a fee from The Haworth Document Delivery Service: 1-800-342-9678. E-mail address: getinfo@haworthpressinc. com <Website: http://www.haworthpressinc.com>]*

KEYWORDS. MTF, transgendered male-to-female youth, social work practice with adolescents, plainclothes transgendered persons

The use of first-person narrative in helping social workers to understand the experiences of transgendered youth has been quite limited. Practitioners solicit the opinions of male-to-female transgendered youth only rarely. First-person accounts offer a unique perspective.

Wendell D. Glenn is Chief of Operations for Gay and Lesbian Adolescent Services (GLASS) in Los Angeles, CA.

[Haworth co-indexing entry note]: "Reflections of an Emerging Male-to-Female Transgendered Consciousness." Glenn, Wendell D. Co-published simultaneously in *Journal of Gay & Lesbian Social Services* (Harrington Park Press, an imprint of The Haworth Press, Inc.) Vol. 10, No. 3/4, 1999, pp. 83-94; and: *Social Services with Transgendered Youth* (ed: Gerald P. Mallon) Harrington Park Press, an imprint of The Haworth Press, Inc., 1999, pp. 83-94. Single or multiple copies of this article are available for a fee from The Haworth Document Delivery Service [1-800-342-9678, 9:00 a.m. - 5:00 p.m. (EST). E-mail address: getinfo@haworthpressinc.com].

Each story of a transgendered person's life is different, unfolding around the particulars of one's life. But listening for the themes and the patterns that emerge from the narrative may help social service professionals (if they are astute listeners) to acquire cues to good practice.

Personal narratives can also offer professionals feedback about how their services are experienced. By creating an open dialogue, these stories allow controversial issues to be addressed more honestly, and harmful practices to be distinguished from helpful ones. The opportunity to tell one's story can be an empowering and healing event. The first-person account also helps shift our attention from pathology to adaptation. When those who literally "live the life" are willing to speak out, they might be better advocates for themselves than professionals, who are usually seen as the experts.

The narratives of those who have emerged wiser or who overcome adversity can be a source of inspiration. The willingness of successful people to discuss their personal experiences publicly is a powerful technique for reducing the stigma attached to the condition of transgenderism.

In acknowledging the pitfalls of first-person narrative, it is also important to keep in mind that the experiences of particular individuals do not necessarily generalize to those of a group as a whole. For narratives to help us understand how to improve services to a population, multiple accounts from varying perspectives, including accounts by transgendered persons at different developmental phases and across a spectrum of cultures, are essential. Only then can we hope to discern universal truths as we design interventions and techniques to help transgendered youth.

Professionals involved in designing approaches to working with transgendered youth must listen to these individual voices for the valuable information that they can share with us. In the narrative below, Wendell Glenn provides us with the gift of a first-person account of his personal experiences as a "plainclothes transgender" person–a term he has coined to define his experiences.

BACK STORY:
THE RECOGNITION
OF A SENSE OF "DIFFERENCE"

"I wonder what kind of dresses we're going to get this time . . . " That was my thought when I was four years old. Actually, what happened is that my mother did domestic work in South Carolina for a white household that gave her hand-me-down children's dresses after she had cleaned for them all day. Then my sisters (I had 7 sisters and 5 brothers) would rummage through the dresses to select the ones they wanted to wear to school. The dresses left over after my sisters selected what they wanted were usually torn or had some flaw which made them inappropriate for school.

My brothers and I used these discarded dresses as pajamas and we all slept in these newfound pajamas. That is, all but my baby brother who just cried and cried and for some reason, unknown to us, he would never wear one of the dresses so . . . he'd sleep in a T-shirt. As for me, I'd sit and wait until the hand-me-down dresses came my way. My other brothers would resist it; they usually slept naked or found some kind of privacy. All of us would sleep in the bed together anyway or on the floor.

When we got a little older, my brothers would rebel and not wear the dresses, but I couldn't wait. I had a little blue one that became my favorite thing to sleep in, but eventually I grew out of it–the dress I mean. I always wondered why I was one brother who was so interested and happy to wear that dress to bed. Around that time I also began to discover that there was a distinct difference between me and my other brothers and other guys my age.

In this first-person narrative, I want to talk about my personal experience as an African American transgender youth growing up in a family that wouldn't even know what a transgender person was. Ironically, my life as a "gender blender" was at first, really glorious. I say that because there were so many people who were fascinated with how I appeared or acted in what I call an external sense. For instance, the little boys who were my favorite friends noticed that I wore really tight pants, or ironed the best creases onto them, or that I always had my hair perfectly slicked. I remember how they used to admire how I used to take my time and groom myself. When the little girls sang "snakes and snails and puppy dog tails," I would sing back "sugar and spice and everything nice," because I really kept up a polished appearance.

I also was the one in class from whom the boys copied answers, the one whose paper they habitually peeked at. Or, if something happened in school, then I'd sometimes take the fall for the boys. I think what I really wanted was the affirmation and attention from them. For me there was even more of a reason than just wanting attention at that particular time. I think that I just enjoyed the intimacy of receiving attention from the males I encountered at the time. The females–the little girls–loved me, because in a lot of ways I was like them and they somehow recognized that in me, but they also saw me as their competition with the boys. Because I was their competition, and yet, was not a biological girl, I overcompensated–I had to be better than them! I made sure that I jumped rope better, or the hopscotch grid I drew on the ground was neater or I hopped on one leg better than the girls. I was always the one who became their best friend and the one who helped them fight when they got in a mess. The prettiest girls, the cheerleaders especially, used my masculinity for protection and what I got in return, was I gravitated toward them as female role-models to emulate.

As a kid coming up in the South, it was fun to go sneak out to the "jook joint" and dance the night away. These places weren't just an "adults-only" environment; children, youths and families were welcomed as well. There was bootleg liquor sold (my mother's secret formula) while a live band played and everybody danced. I remember being in the middle of the room–being the center of attention. People looking at me and loving everything I did. I felt great happiness there. My community looked at me as a treasure because I was a performer, a chameleon . . . the older guys threw quarters or patted me on the butt and the girls always wanted me to dance with them.

I stood out. There was a goodness about me. "Look at the way he walks," people would say. But for me there was always a sense of protection. Part of the external was so celebrated by everybody around me that I didn't really know that I was different because I was so busy being happy and making everyone else happy.

As I got older, and ventured into other communities outside of the one that protected me, I found myself sticking with my own community–with my own people. I had so much in common with these folks. The poverty that we all lived in, made us all stick together. In the cold winters we helped each other and in the spring we worked together or cut wood for the next winter. So I really didn't have time to look at who was different or what made you look different or act different because we were so busy dealing with survival.

This changed once I started to mingle with people from neighboring areas. I can remember when I was in the first grade in an all-black school, being there with my peer group, but also for the first time, I was clustered along with some of these outsiders. That was the first time I started hearing comments like, "Look at him, he walks funny." That's when they started calling me "sissy" and all those hurtful names. They recognized my "difference" and unlike the people in my community–it mattered to them. So it was an amazing feeling to have felt so celebrated by my community and then all of a sudden to be so ridiculed when I came into contact with outsiders. Some of the people from my community began to protect me but others began to align themselves with the outsiders and for the first time, they began to look at my "difference," too. These were the same people I performed for or was celebrated by–and yet, now they only saw my "difference" where they once saw a fun member of their community. It was at this juncture, that the internal dilemma started to kick in. It was right around the first or second grade.

I realize now, although, obviously I didn't at the time, that it's most important that a transgender-oriented person struggling with peer group identification receives the support and the encouragement of parents, or an aunt or family member that he or she can count on for a support system. There were days I went home from school crying because I hurt so bad. But remember, once I was back in the community, I was still the performer for everybody. No one expected me to cry and so I had to put on this front. Most of the negative part that I was feeling, most of the stuff that was going on and burning inside of me internally, was now hidden. That same person that performed for you was really a very isolated and lonely boy. Who was I going to tell? Who was I going to go to? There was no one else that I could identify who was like me. And, I really couldn't even articulate or communicate what was going on.

This sense of isolation and loneliness is one of the reasons that transgendered people have such a hard time with socialization. It is only when they become healthy adults or healthy-thinking people that they start to build their own support systems. It is at this period of time that parents really need to become that particular force in their child's life, but most parents are clueless, because they expect their children to be heterosexual, not gay or lesbian, and certainly not transgendered. What would be so helpful is if the parents could pick up some of that misery that is paining that child. To identify, speak to it, to get help for it. But, unfortunately, most parents are ill-equipped to care for a transgendered child. Fortunately, even though she was not armed with the proper information to deal with my transgendered identity, I did have a mother who I could go to. It would always be a different story about what I was sad about, but I knew enough to never tell her about the real thing, because again, not only didn't I know how to communicate what the "difference" felt like, but even then I didn't have the words for it. But nonetheless, I began to hate how I felt and in some ways to hate myself as well.

In my case, I was a typical child of the Deep South growing up in a large family with a single parent, my mother. And even though my mother was one of the most nurturing and loving parents that anyone could ever have, and still is–she wasn't experienced enough with gender issues to assess or look at what I was going through at that time. So I have long since gotten over any blaming behavior or saying, "Why didn't you do this?" or "Why didn't you do that?" My mother did the best she could with 12 children, but she simply was not prepared in any way to deal with her child who was transgendered.

There were other factors as well–especially in light of the fact that the Church was so important in our everyday life. Not only did everybody know me in the community, but everybody went to the same church. During sermons, the preacher was openly condemning–I mean very openly condemning about women going with women, men going with men, and for me at the time, going to church was the worst time of my life because every time I left feeling ridiculed and harassed. And what really got to me was that some of these people who threw quarters at me or patted me on the butt in the jook joint on Saturday night, looked at me like I was the worst thing in the world on Sunday in church.

So it was all of these mixed messages, mixed feelings, mixed emotions that I went through that were balled up like a volcano that doesn't erupt. Most of the time I felt incredibly isolated. But I also overcompensated for the inadequacy I felt inside. I overexerted myself. I did this because I was so desperate, so busy trying to fit in–especially trying to fit into the Church. In the church I joined the choir. Or, in school I tried to get on the football team. I tried so hard to be good that when I came home from school, I did extra chores or whatever it took to make sure I compensated for all the loss I felt internally.

Balancing Internal and External Factors

In looking at the internal facets and external facets, although they run neck and neck, I realized that there has to be some type of balance. There is always a struggle between trying to feel good about yourself internally and having that supported externally. In my own family, I think that my brothers and sisters always knew there was something different about me. But again, we were in survival mode, a close-knit family, but struggling to survive poverty. So it was not something that we openly discussed. It wasn't that they looked at or saw a "difference," but they did perceive difference. In many ways, they knew, but we never talked about it. I was the son who was beside my mother for hours and hours in the kitchen, who would just look at her cook and then begin to learn to do it myself. I even learned to prepare meals better than some of my sisters. So that was classified as "He's flaunting," or "he's going to be a chef." An extra hand in the kitchen didn't hurt. So . . . I made lots of compromises. Most of the compromises that I did make entailed always being available to lend a hand to someone else being more happy, and so, my happiness became derived from someone else's.

Becoming a teenager changed everything for me. Going into the teen stage, when teenagers want to date and be intimate with each other, caused the struggle between internal and external to worsen. It was at this time that I began to bring out some of what was happening to me internally, to the external world. When I look back on the days in high school, there were a couple, two or three others, of the same orientation. There's a comfort in finding others like you, you kind of seek each other out. When you meet another person like you–you know when another person is identifying like you–there's a certain look, it's a feeling. That's why the transfamily has become so popular because you really do begin to form a family, to know each other, once you find your people.

This was the time that some of the guys in our community started to wear dresses to school–It was different than pajamas just to wear at night! But to wear the lipstick and wear the dresses to school is when the guys who felt this way started to say internally, "I cannot take it anymore, I need to play this out, I need to express this." I never dressed in women's clothes at school and usually I became alienated from my friends who did this. They caught a lot of heat. But I was different. For me, it wasn't the way I *looked or dressed*, it was the way I *felt*. It's who I *was*, it's how I identified at that particular time inside.

"For Colored Girls Only . . . "

During the adolescent period of development, some of the transgender psychosocial aspects begin to manifest themselves externally. Some of the same teenagers who were my age, and had gender issues, began to dress in the clothing of the opposite gender. A few of them were actually accepted and respected, but only on certain occasions. This clear change on their part, became a predicament for me. Even at a young age I always believed there were certain limitations to my internal feelings of femaleness. I was a great believer in blending in, being comfortable with who I was, but not sticking out like a sore thumb. When I mention the transgender psychosocial aspects, I mean first and foremost, the loneliness. And I mean loneliness in a way where your peer group becomes very narrow, very small, and you can almost predict the one or two people who you can secretly talk to. Some of those same guys who, when you were younger, celebrated you, at this point have this straight macho-type image and you become ridiculed by them. I remember thinking to myself at this time–"You're crazy." "You're a crazy faggot or even worse." These were some of the same guys who behind closed doors are waiting to have a sexual run-in with you. And after that, when they saw you again in public, they didn't want to be bothered.

The girls at this particular time started seriously looking at me as "the competition." Or some of the girls whom I knew I could talk to at this time, would use me to talk to my brothers who were active in sports because they liked them. So they would use me to approach them. Or they would allow me to be friends with them because they knew I could fight and keep jealous girls off of them.

All in all, although I socialized, these relationships were not genuine friendships. I was used by people to get what they wanted. It's a type of loneliness that cut me to the core, the message was clear–stay in the closet! We will take you out, when and if we need you for something, to entertain us, to do something for us, or to defend us. Who was I going to go to when I needed something? It was a question I asked my self repeatedly over those years. The reality was–there wasn't any support system. There wasn't anybody there for me. Apart from this loneliness, I felt shame. Guilt started setting in because I began to wonder if I had become a failure to myself and my family. I guess if I had a healthy self-perception at this point, I would have begun to build on where I was and set goals and just go further and move on. But I realized that this is what it was, that this is what my life was worth and I had to either sink or swim. Fortunately, I decided to swim–meaning that I made peace with myself and my transgender orientation, and set about beginning to actualize myself professionally. And I'm still swimming.

When I really again began to realize who I was, and whether or not that deviated from everyone else, I realized too that I was no different than anybody else. I was a person–a human–with feelings. I wanted love, I wanted to belong, I was an emotional person who had needs and those needs were not so different from other people's needs. It was society that began to color me crazy–not my transgendered nature. I had ridiculed myself for too long about hiding my feelings. My feelings were real and could no longer be denied. Not only do *we* look different to *them*, but *they* look different to *us*. So there had to be a sense of give and take, compromise, if you will, but not just on my part.

For me the "shame game" was a sport I decided I wasn't going to play. I could not be a part of the "shame game." I realized early on that the "shame game" will destroy you. My guilt was an inner guilt, not rooted in whether or not I was successful in the eyes of family and friends, or whether or not I was a failure to them, but whether I was successful to myself. Although this was a time of great personal transformation, it was also a time of great depression, which comes mainly from the stress of wanting people to buy into who you are. You want people not to look at you as if you are unusual. And you begin to look for this particular love and acceptance. Sometimes it leads you to all the wrong places–right into substance abuse, manipulating, stealing . . . behavior that's unacceptable. I've been there, done that. I would have done anything to be loved by someone or accepted by someone, be it family or not.

At this time, those of us who feel tortured do not seek out support systems, support groups or counseling or therapy, but instead opt for "home remedies"–to enable ourselves to get better and move on. Such "remedies" could lead right into some point of suicide, substance abuse, risk-taking; all of which makes us a very vulnerable population. There's a saying that, "you have to stand for something or you'll fall for anything." At this point, the yearning for meaningful human contact is so strong that we can literally fall for anything.

"Color Me Crazy"

Trying to find a true, healthy identity of self within the context of a transgender identity is difficult. Most of the confusion and frustration about who I was stemmed from my own peer group and I mean my transgendered peer group! There is a point of view that is guided solely by the physical attributes one has, as compared with what one has from the opposite sex. Transgendered people are constantly comparing and criticizing each other in the area of *looks*. Whether or not you can pass as a woman (or a man in the case of FTMs) becomes the main focus of survival and preoccupation. REALNESS is everything! Your level of acceptance is determined by how well you are able to hide your penis (known as tucking) to make it appear as if it were a vagina. There is also a high outlay of energy placed on the art of putting on makeup, making sure to cover up razor bumps, battling unwanted hair growth, or making sure you are crafty enough to fix your chest to present just the right breast size. This process becomes a preoccupation for some and so much a part of every day routine for others that it is normal grooming. Day after day, night after night, life becomes an interchangeable transformation and only when it is time to sleep, and you pull off the mask making sure not to look in a mirror or you could be horrified of the physical reality–does it all come off.

As a young adult MTF transgender life is most crazy making. It is especially crazy if you are a career-oriented individual with goals in mind. For example, if you are scheduled to work at 8 a.m., you have to allow enough time to fix yourself up. Fixing yourself up could consist of anything from propping your wig or hair weave correctly, to making sure you are taking the right hormone pill or shot.

It is a rarity, pure luck and a blessing, when a transgendered person becomes successful outside of the world that they create for themselves. This world of the MTF transgender involves everybody meeting together at each other's homes. Getting together for house parties, or hanging out in the private homes of others who are part of the transfamily, involves the same activities as others are involved in: cooking a dinner, scheming about the latest juicy gossip, sewing clothes, and just plain old having fun.

Another means of socializing, as well as a way of making life meaningful is hanging out at the local gay bars. Many of "the girls" (the familiar for MTFs) are able to perform on stage and show off their latest fashions. The bar becomes symbolic of a newly created family system–the transfamily. With a mixture of gay, lesbian, bi- and questioning individuals, the transgender person is still the most ridiculed and misunderstood, but at the same time admired for her performance.

Again, the performer is revered, the real person rejected. After the performance, you become a thing, or the subject of the next joke waiting to be told.

Relational issues are always questionable. There is always the feeling of whether or not the person is relating to me or relating to the person I have created. I have seen friends who are "bent down" (passable as another gender) destroy themselves over the fact that they have fallen in love with a man who does not know the "T" (true gender identity). The stresses of depression and suicidal ideation, hopelessness, despair, low self-esteem, as well as vulnerability to crimes, violence, drugs, and risky health behaviors are all revisited periodically throughout the lives of transgendered people.

"Keeping My Craziness Within"

A "plain clothes" transgender, the category that fits me, seems to blend into the framework of normalcy in American lifestyles. If you take away the lipstick, the padding, the female clothing, the modulation in voice, the change in name and pronoun use, what is left is the same person. The only difference is that this person becomes more acceptable to others, and with luck, to themselves. We are acceptable to the larger social world, because we "fit in." The "plainclothes" transgender and what I term "the fixed/prepared" transgender both are the same internally. The only thing that keeps us apart, and makes us different is the terminology. Terminology that is either created by us, or by society. There are, of course, some actual differences also. First and most importantly, "plainclothes" transgender persons are permitted to move in and out–to circulate if you will, amongst all of the genders through "acceptable" eyes–again, because we "fit in." We are sometimes erroneously viewed as closeted by both gay and straight society. "Plainclothes" transgenders, because we are invisible to most, are usually more employable and find it easier to have access to membership with groups that have societal approval–the gym, the church, and fraternities. In the gay bar, the "plainclothes" transgenders are part of the audience, not part of the performance. After the show, the individual really does exist. Although this "plainclothes" individual is even more misunderstood than the average transgender, they are generally healthier internally.

The nurturing support and relationship connections from one's family permits the plainclothes transgender to be more equipped to function in the world, systematically without the physical barriers that many "fixed/prepared" transgenders face. Relational issues are more feasible because what you see is what you get. Like our fixed/prepared MTF counterparts, the plainclothes transgender person is intimately attracted to heterosexual men–men who recognize the women in us, without the additional paraphernalia of female clothing, make-up and other accouterments. Most plainclothes transgender persons do not date, and are not interested in dating, gay men. The men whom we date are also more comfortable being seen with us in public, as the experiences that intimately bond us are internal and therefore, undetectable to the average person.

Whether plainclothes or fix/prepared, transgendered persons are some of the most ambitious people on the face of this earth. Part of our problem is, "How do we get there?" No one has actually devised programs for third gender populations to advance themselves, socially, economically, or politically. Although there are some unique needs within this population, most of us want the same things that everyone else wants–respect, a decent living wage, affordable housing, adequate health care, and people around us who really care about us. We have yet to see a legislative body or social program with the mandate and the agenda to adequately serve this population. Optimistic as I am, I do not believe that in my lifetime we will see that, but we must learn to work to take care of our own people.

Group Work Practice with Transgendered Male to Female Sex Workers

Rebecca Klein

SUMMARY. Group work is frequently the method of choice for working with adolescents. This paper focuses on group work with transgendered youth who engage in sex work. Utilizing case examples, this paper provides an overview of the role that sex work plays in the lives of some transgendered youth and offers guidance for those interested in utilizing group work approaches with transgendered adolescents. *[Article copies available for a fee from The Haworth Document Delivery Service: 1-800-342-9678. E-mail address: getinfo@haworthpressinc.com <Website: http:// www.haworthpressinc.com>]*

KEYWORDS. Transgendered youth, group work practice with transgendered youth, sex workers

INTRODUCTION

The practice of group work with adolescent transgendered sex workers represents a complex area for innovation by social service providers. This paper examines the nature of group work and its relevance to issues facing transgendered youth who engage in sex work. Social service providers interested in this type of practice will need a

Rebecca Klein is a group worker at Green Chimneys Children's Services in New York City.

[Haworth co-indexing entry note]: "Group Work Practice with Transgendered Male to Female Sex Workers." Klein, Rebecca. Co-published simultaneously in *Journal of Gay & Lesbian Social Services* (Harrington Park Press, an imprint of The Haworth Press, Inc.) Vol. 10, No. 3/4, 1999, pp. 95-109; and: *Social Services with Transgendered Youth* (ed: Gerald P. Mallon) Harrington Park Press, an imprint of The Haworth Press, Inc., 1999, pp. 95-109. Single or multiple copies of this article are available for a fee from The Haworth Document Delivery Service [1-800-342-9678, 9:00 a.m. - 5:00 p.m. (EST). E-mail address: getinfo@haworthpressinc.com].

working definition for transgender, as well as an awareness of the impact of the term "prostitute" before doing this work.

The term transgender covers a broad range of gender non-conforming identities and behaviors, including transsexuals (preoperative, postoperative, and persons who are interested in gender reassignment surgery), transvestites, male and female impersonators (Drag Kings/ Queens) and "gender benders" (persons who overtly challenge gender norms for cultural and political reasons) (Ryan & Futterman, 1998). Transgendered persons may be heterosexual, homosexual, bisexual, or asexual. These categories of gender expression offer a general framework for the ways in which transgendered young people may express their gender identity.

For the purpose of this paper I will not use the term "prostitute" to describe the behavior of this population. "Prostitute" is too simplistic and may not accurately identify the experiences of young people who engage in selling sex (McMullen, 1986). There is also an implied moral judgment attached to the term, which I would caution practitioners to avoid. The young sex workers do not favor, for the most part, the label "prostitute." Femme queen, sex worker, and hustler are some of the words commonly used by the youth themselves and which are defined in the appendix. Young people engaged in prostitution often deny their involvement in this practice. Adopting an alternative term helps to minimize societal stigmatization associated with being a "prostitute."

As one 17-year-old boy states:

> I dress up in drags when I go out, I pump down to the pier in high heels, a wig, and a dress. I'm a femme queen so I go to the Femme Queen Stroll.

Before addressing the implications for group work, it is necessary to understand the thought process behind why a young person enters into "sex work," and the specific circumstances which make it more likely for a transgendered young person to become a sex worker. Existing literature focuses on the high correlation between experiences of early sexual abuse and entry into "sex work." However, there are other factors which should be taken into consideration. Socioeconomic factors, job opportunities and employable skills, education, psychosocial development, familial support, and ethnicity, are some of the contributing factors which may need to be addressed. One can not simply infer from a young boy or girl's previous abuse history that this is the only defining reason for entry into sex work. A young person entering into sex work is most likely to have something which is lacking in their physical, emotional, and spiritual self.

Transgendered persons face discrimination in employment, education, housing and health care. Society is less accepting of gender-atypical behavior expressed by boys than by girls. Transgendered young men, particularly those who are gender non-conforming, are frequently the targets of verbal and physical violence. Lack of familial support leads many transgendered youth to drop out of school, leave home, ending up on the streets where they are at risk for drug abuse, HIV and prostitution (Ryan & Futterman, 1998).

Literature Review

Currently, there is a lack of professional literature surrounding group work with adolescent trangendered youth and in particular those who engage in sex work. The literature which does exist (Anderson, Freese, & Pennbridge, 1994; Boles & Elifson, 1994; Pleak & Meyer-Bahlburg, 1990; Rotheram-Borus et al., 1994) focuses on the sexual behaviors, and knowledge of AIDS among adolescent gay male prostitutes.

Coleman (1989) provides a discussion of the psychosocial development of adolescent gay and bisexual males who prostitute, and attributes this behavior to numerous factors including socio-economic status, family characteristics, previous history of abuse, drug abuse, and sexual orientation. McMullen's (1987) focal point is about the relationship of power between the customer and sex worker. The literature on transvestite prostitutes has highlighted this population's risk for HIV infection (Elifson et al., 1993).

Exploration of the diagnostic category Gender Identity Disorder is at the forefront of most of the professional literature surrounding transgendered youth (American Psychiatric Association, 1995). The discussion of interventions and treatments for transgendered youth, including the need to create an environment of acceptance which helps these youth clarify their identity confusion, and resolve conflict, is the focus of Ryan and Futterman's (1998) discussion on the topic.

Highlighted in the sections that follow are several of the key issues pertaining to transgendered youth.

Homelessness and Institutionalization

Whether the adolescent leaves home or is forced out, he or she often enters into foster care or social service systems, where he or she is at risk for further discrimination, neglect, harassment, and violence. It is not uncommon for a transgendered youth to view the streets as a safer environment (Mallon, 1998a).

A 16-year-boy in a New York City group home for youth states:

> In my other group home, I would stay out all night and make coins (money). It was so bad there (group home) that I would always AWOL and go to the "stroll." Staff and residents would beat me up and take my money, because I was gay. I had this one "date" who would let me stay at his house whenever I wanted to leave the group home. I would stay there and then go back to my group home with money and new clothes.

For many of these young persons in foster care, inadequately trained staff members often allow the abuse to continue. In other cases, it is tacitly condoned because of staff's own bias against transgendered youth. The cases where these youth have been discarded by their families and the social service system make them vulnerable for sexual exploitation. Survival sex becomes a necessity when these neglected teens attempt to provide food, clothing and shelter for themselves where the system has failed to protect them. Transgendered youth have also been victims of forced/inappropriate psychiatric hospitalizations because in some areas of the country gender identity disorder is viewed as a correctable condition (see Soblinski, 1997 for a graphic account of this experience).

Education Life Skills/Employment

Lack of education, employable skills, and job opportunities for transgendered youth contribute to their entry into sex work. Transgendered youth, unlike gay and lesbian adolescents, are more frequently abused in schools because they do not or cannot conform to traditional cultural expectations of feminine or masculine behavior. Regardless of their sexual orientation, their visibility often leads to scapegoating, harassment, and persistent verbal abuse from peers. In many cases, the harassment turns to physical violence. Transgendered teens are often forced out of their schools, because of ignorance and hatred (Mallon, 1997).

As one 16-year-old male to female transgendered youth states:

> I just stopped going to school. One year I was a boy, and then the next, I looked and talked like a girl.

> They didn't know what to do with me, they were scared. I have no problem with who I am. But they did.

Because positive interaction with peers may be lacking for these youth, opportunities to develop appropriate interpersonal social skills may also be limited.

Victimization and Trauma

Physical and sexual abuse among teenage hustlers has been linked to the practice of sex work (Coleman, 1989). Studies of female prostitutes have indicated a strong association between early sexual victimization and sex work involvement (Boyer & James, 1983; James, 1980; James & Meyerding, 1979; Silbert, 1980).

Feelings of being unimportant to anyone or anything, are not uncommon among young hustlers (McMullen, 1987). Statements such as "I don't care what happens," or "If it happens, it happens, who cares?" highlight these extreme feelings of hopelessness and helplessness which are often associated with depression or other serious mental health conditions.

A sense of worthlessness, low self-esteem, and social isolation are also associated with the societal discrimination against gender nonconforming young people. Other circumstances that contribute to this are lower socio-economic status, ethnicity, and limited resources, which lead these youth towards sex work.

There is a high incidence of rape and sexual assault among this population, which often goes unreported. Fear of being abused a second time by the police prevents transgendered youth from reporting these incidents. The comments of this 19-year-old corroborate this:

> I guess I don't care about myself, I'll let my "date" have sex with me without a condom. Nothing's swollen, I don't have the shakes, so I think I'm fine. Who cares, it's more money that way.

Still another young person recalls his history of sexual abuse this way:

> Ya know, I was sexually abused when I was little. And I think about that sometimes when I'm out on the stroll, but I don't think it has anything to do with why I do it. Where else can I make three hundred dollars in a night?

Some youth reported being abused by the very adults who are supposed to protect them:

> I was on the stroll last night, and this cop stopped me. He made me get into the car and said he would arrest me if I didn't give him a blow job. I ended up having sex with him, because I was scared he'd arrest me. I just looked at his badge sitting there around his neck.

Drug and Alcohol Abuse

Alcohol and drug abuse are pervasive among this population, which further increases their risk for violence and sexually transmitted diseases (STDs). It is not uncommon for drugs to be used as a payment for sex (Coleman, 1989). Young sex workers will often use drugs or alcohol while hustling because of the lowering of inhibitions, and because substances "numb" the body and spirit. Addiction to drugs and alcohol contributes or permits others to continue in sex work. One 17-year-old Latino youth provided this account of using substances:

> Before I go to the stroll, I get high, I smoke a blunt or two. It makes it easier. I don't have to think about or feel what's happening to me.

Young people are frequently expected to use drugs or alcohol as a part of the "date":

> Sometimes I'll have a "date" and he will want me to snort coke with him or he'll get me drunk. I'm usually already high so I just go along with whatever he wants.

Group Work Approach

The group work approach allows members to identify together activities that will strengthen their functioning within the group and the larger society. The special resource of group work is mutual aid, which is the assistance members provide to one another (Gitterman & Schulman, 1994). Through the examples of others, members learn about themselves, as they share the commonalities of their experience and feel the connection to their peers. The positive achievements provide group members with direction and feelings of hope about the future.

The discussion of sexuality in group work with adolescents is a vital area which needs to be addressed (Malekoff, 1997) and an area that social workers need additional training and support to explore. Beyond the physical aspects of sex, adolescents need to be a given the space to understand and express their feelings and experiences. Discussions and activities focused around sex work, like other taboo subjects (i.e., homosexuality, pregnancy) are likely to evoke anxiety (Malekoff, 1997) in the youth and in some cases in the professional. Patience, flexibility, and sensitivity are necessary in dealing with the anxiety and resistance surrounding discussion or activities related to sex work. For example, a social worker needs to be aware when addressing this issue, that a young person may be resistant to attending the group based only on the group's name. Therefore advertising the group with an appropriate name is key. Our group at the agency where I completed my Field Instruction was called Stroller's Anonymous–a group for youth who wished to stop engaging in sex work.

The resistance to social services by adolescent transgendered sex workers is caused in large part by the societal discrimination and stigma which plagues this population, or the fear that they will be treated as less than human. Social workers should be aware of how these factors affect their work. The unique challenge to group work practice is to facilitate a group process that centers on strengthening the potential for growth, belonging, and health, as group members reach out to each other and to a world that extends beyond the boundaries of the group (Schwartz, 1976).

Strategies for Effective Interventions

Because the sparse literature which deals with the needs of transgendered youth focuses on gender non-conforming behavior as a pathology (American Psychological Association, 1994, pp. 40-41), most social workers have very limited information about how to work with a transgendered youth. Social workers are not immune to the societal stigma surrounding "sex work," and to the ideology that gender non-conforming behavior is a mental illness. As such, workers must assess their own feelings about transgendered youth who engage in sex work and assess their own level of comfort for talking about sensitive subject matter. Social workers need to educate themselves about the needs and issues that affect this population. They must also remind themselves that it is a basic premise of social work practice to meet their client where they are. Making assumptions that their client is confused and will grow out of this "stage," or worse yet, that the youth is simply engaging in attention-seeking behavior by taking part in gender non-conforming behavior, is dangerous, and will affect the level of trust that will or will not form within the therapeutic relationship. It is inappropriate and unethical for social workers to project their personal beliefs, as well as traditional society's views regarding gender identity and sex work, onto these youth.

Group work services to transgendered adolescent sex workers should address practical issues, such as education and employment, life skill development, dealing with issues of oppression, and identity issues. The complexity of attempting to "pass" as one's preferred gender, the struggle of obtaining and sustaining "legitimate" work, learning to relate to peers and adults in a non-sexualized manner, are all topics that should be introduced.

By normalizing non-conforming gender expression and the learned behavior of sex work, group work begins to break down the taboos surrounding this population. The worker creates a safe, non-judgmental environment focusing on empowerment and peer support. Addressing the more practical aspects that this population deals with alleviates the pressure and the focus on discussing their experiences while hustling, which are deeply embedded with feelings of shame and mistrust.

The most important factor for social workers to address when working with clients who are transgendered sex workers is that the worker must be supportive of the adolescent, and must feel comfortable with the issues of homosexuality, transgenderism, and sexuality in general, including the therapist's own feelings about sexuality (Mallon, 1994).

Case Illustration

Shame is a prevalent feeling that often hinders the group members from sharing the experiences they had while hustling. Fear of judgment, rejection, and exposure create anxiety for the members when sharing their sex work activities. The following case example provides illustrations of group work practice with adolescent sex workers. Highlighted is an example from a group which is led by the author at Green Chimneys Children's Services, a 25-bed residential program for gay, bisexual, and transgendered youth within the New York City foster care system.

The group is composed of eight members. The group members self-identify as gay, bisexual, transgendered, and questioning. The youth are either African American or Latino. Two of the members identify as transgendered or "femme queen" (i.e., strong desire to express themselves as the opposite gender); the others identify as butch queens (i.e., occasionally cross-dress, no strong desire to live as opposite gender, mannerisms tend to be "effeminate" but most often are hypermasculine). Each of these categories deviates from the gender norms within our society. Butch queen and femme queen are categories of identification commonly found in the African American and Latino subculture of the gay community. Each member can be categorized as what Maloney (1974) calls a *street hustler*. There were varying levels of sex work activity at the time the group met, ranging from inactive to nightly.

The following excerpt of the group process begins with one member sharing his experiences of working out on the "stroll," and his feelings around his behaviors. This prompts another member to speak about the shame and anger he has about being out on the stroll. The worker makes use of group feedback to maximize the sharing of different experiences about the feelings of shame and mistrust. The worker validates the members' experiences and creates an environment of non-judgment. Group members benefit from each other's shared experiences.

Manny begins telling the group that when he used to go out on the stroll he did it because he felt badly about himself, and it was self-destructive. He went on to say that before, when he was depressed in the house, he would get dressed up in drag, get high, and go out on the stroll.

> Manny: When I was out on the stroll I wasn't depressed anymore, I felt beautiful, like a real woman. But when I would come home I would be depressed again and feel dirty. This is why I sometimes didn't come home.

Chris: I know when I'm out on the stroll I feel sexy, like I have power, even though I know it's not true.

Terrence: Yeah, you feel like you have power, because it's all these white men coming to me for sex, but really it's they who have the control, cuz I don't know what they might do to me. When I come home I sometimes have to take two showers because I feel so dirty.

(The group members nod in agreement with Terrence.)

Worker: It seems like you are all agreeing with Terrence and the feeling of being scared and ashamed.

Jose: That's why I don't like to talk about this. I'm not proud of doing it, but I do.

Victor: I'm embarrassed about hustling, too, but until I find a job that will pay as much, I will keep doing it.

Jose: Yeah, I want that job, too, but I don't know if I can keep doing it. I just feel so bad about myself.

Manny: I've had so much happen to me while I was on the stroll. I've been raped, beaten up, arrested.

(The group members again nod in agreement)

Victor: But, you know, it's not just about the money. It's also about trying to be real also. I mean, if a man will pay for you, then you must be real.

Worker: You're all sharing about similar feelings and experiences. It sounds like you've been through a lot of terrible things, and you are still here today and have been able to survive. It takes a lot of strength and courage to share your experiences with others.

Implications for Group Work Practice

The following suggestions may be helpful for social workers dealing with this population:

1. In addition to being understanding, empathic, and providing a non-judgmental environment, when counseling these young

people, professionals need to possess accurate information regarding both transgendered youth and adolescent sex workers.

2. A basic principle of social work practice states that practitioners should meet their clients where they are. Let your client know that being transgendered is okay, and that it is okay to explore their gender identity, if fact, it is okay for them to go back and forth in their gender identification. Regarding their involvement in sex work, let your clients know that you do not judge them whether they continue or stop doing sex work. Let them know that you will support them regardless of their involvement in sex work.

3. Help your clients to understand and clarify their feelings about their gender identity and their sex work practice.

4. The social worker should be able to provide accurate and age appropriate information, which is readable and understandable, to the young person. Currently literature for and about transgendered youth and adolescent sex workers is limited. Both the social worker and group members together can seek out resources, which offer information to assist the young person in abolishing myths and stereotypes. Movies, both fictional and documentary, such as–"My Own Private Idaho" "Black Is Black Ain't," "Ma Vie en Rose" and "Paris Is Burning" (Livingston, 1991; Van Sant, 1991)–which explore the nature of the experiences of male sex workers and the transgendered experience–are helpful educational tools for facilitating group discussions.

5. Help clients to develop appropriate contacts within the transgendered and the youth community. Social workers should educate themselves about these resources and be able to refer clients to them. Workers should also be prepared, at least for the first interview, to accompany youth to these resources for support. Agencies within the gay, lesbian, and bisexual community frequently offer services to this population.

6. Help clients to develop effective interpersonal coping mechanisms to deal with the negative effects of societal stigmatization. Assist young people in exploring and developing mechanisms to deal with conflict, clarify identity confusion, relationships, depression, safer sex, and peer pressures.

7. Be aware of the signs of suicidal ideation, alcohol and other substance abuse. Know resources to which clients can be referred to for services.

8. Social workers should assist their clients in clarifying identity confusion, and whether or not they are appropriate candidates for hormone therapy. Social workers should educate themselves on the appropriate resources available for hormone therapy in accredited health care settings, with trained health care practitioners.

9. Social workers should discuss the young person's feelings and concerns associated with dressing in gender preference clothing.

10. Social workers should be prepared to advocate for a young person who is having trouble at school, in a group or foster home, on the streets or in their own families. The protection of these youth is an important task for the social worker.

11. Respect confidentiality at all times. The relationship must be based on trust, understanding, and respect.

CONCLUSION

Groups that deal with teenage sex work as well as adolescent sexuality need to be provided by social workers. Groups that encourage the verbal expression of all the various forms that sexuality can take need to be accessible to youth. It is important for social workers to validate transgendered youth and their experiences within society. The sharing of experiences and feelings within groups through discussion or structured activities (i.e., watching movies, art projects, and reading) facilitates the adolescent's development of decision making and interpersonal skills. In addition, the group provides support for these young people around education, employment, safer sex, relationships, dating, and gender identity issues.

The dearth of literature on transgendered youth in social work and the limited discussion of this content in social work education must be addressed by educators and practitioners in the years ahead. All too frequently, discussions of adolescent human sexuality, if they occur at all, focus almost exclusively on heterosexuality. Practitioners and policy-makers must challenge each other to confront the larger spectrum of sexual identities. The social work profession must address the issue of transgendered prostitution in its literature and its services. The acknowledgment that adolescent male and transgendered sex workers exist is a first step. Service providers, in and out of the gay, lesbian, bisexual, and transgendered communities, must communicate areas of need and contribute their insight and practice experience to the literature.

Social service providers also can not assume that young persons coming for help want to stop their sex work practice. Social workers must offer an environment that is free from judgment and personal bias. By practicing one of the basic tenets of social work practice, meeting their clients where they are, practitioners can begin to provide services which address the unique needs of these adolescents. Social services for transgendered youth should include nutritional services (balanced meals), shelter services (either permanent or temporary, to provide a safe environment from the streets and other hostile environments), educational services, employment training, sensitive health care, individual and group counseling, case management to assist in advocating for benefits and clients' rights, appropriate referral for drug and alcohol treatment, and recreational activities.

Group work practice with transgendered teens involved in selling sex opens the door by acknowledging the existence of sex work, and helps to normalize the group members' experiences. The group members begin to see that they are not alone and that others have had similar experiences and feelings. It is necessary that the social work profession begin to address these issues. Future work must begin by providing concrete services to these youth as well as developing therapeutic relationships with them.

REFERENCES

American Psychiatric Association. (1994). *Diagnostic and statistical manual of mental disorders (4th ed.)*. Washington, DC: p. 180-183.

Anderson, J., Freese, T., & Pennbridge, J. (1994). Sexual risk behavior and condom use among street youth in Hollywood. *Family Planning Perspectives, 26*(1), 22-25.

Berliner, A. (Director) (1997) *Ma Vie en Rose*. Los Angeles, SONY Classics.

Boles, J., & Elifson, K. (1994). Sexual identity and HIV: The male prostitute. *Journal of Sex Research, 31*(1), 39-46.

Boyer, D. (1989). Male prostitution and homosexual identity. In G. Herdt (Ed.), *Gay and lesbian youth* (pp. 151-184). New York: Haworth Press.

Boyer, D. & James, J. (1983). Prostitutes as victims: Sex and social order. In D.E.J.

Mc Namara & A. Karman (Eds.), *Deviants: Victims or victimizers* (pp. 109-146) NY: Haworth Press.

Cates, J. A. (1989). Adolescent male prostitution by choice. *Child and Adolescent Social Work*, *6*(2), 151-157.

Coleman, E. (1989). The development of male prostitution activity among gay and bisexual adolescents. In G. Herdt (Ed.), *Gay and lesbian youth* (pp. 131-149). New York: Haworth Press.

Dixon, D., & Dixon, J. (1998). SHE-MALE prostitutes: Who are they, what do they do, and why do they do it? In J. Elias, V. Bullough, V. Elias, & G. Brewer (Eds.), *Prostitution: On whores, hustlers, and johns* (pp. 260-266). New York: Prometheus Books.

Getzel, G. (1998). Group work practice with gay men and lesbians. In G. Mallon (Ed.), *Foundations of social work practice with lesbian and gay persons* (pp. 131-143). New York: Harrington Park Press.

Gitterman, A., & Shulman, L. (1994). The life model, mutual aid, oppression, and the mediating function. In A. Gitterman and L. Shulman (Eds.), *Mutual aid groups, vulnerable populations and the life cycle* (pp. 3-28). New York: Columbia University Press.

James, J. (1980). *Entrance into juvenile prostitution*. Final Report to the National Institutes of Mental Health (Grant No. 29968). Seattle, WA: University of Washington Department of Psychiatry and Behavioral Sciences.

James, J., & Meyerding, J. (1979). Early sexual experience as a factor in prostitution. *Archives of Sexual Behavior*, *7*(1), 31-42.

Jesson, J. (1993). Understanding adolescent female prostitution: A literature review. *British Journal of Social Work*, *23*, 517-530.

Livingston, J. (Director) (1991). *Paris Is Burning*. [Film].

Malekoff, A. (1997). Adolescent sexuality and group work. In A. Malekoff (Ed.), *Group work with adolescents: Principles and practice* (pp. 242-266). New York: Guilford Press.

Mallon, G. (1994). Counseling strategies with gay and lesbian youth. In T. DeCrescenzo (Ed.), *Helping gay and lesbian youth: New policies, new programs, new practice* (pp. 75-91). New York: Haworth Press.

Mallon, G. (1998). *We don't exactly get the welcome wagon: The experience of gay and lesbian adolescents in child welfare systems*. New York: Columbia University Press.

Mallon, G.P. (1997). When schools are not safe places: Gay, lesbian, bisexual, and transgendered young people in educational settings. *Reaching Today's Youth*, *2*(1), 41-45.

Maloney, P. (1980). *Street hustling: Growing up gay*. Unpublished manuscript.

McMullen, R. (1987). Boys involved in prostitution. *Youth and Policy*, Winter, 12-19.

McMullen, R. (1987). Youth prostitution: A balance of power. *Journal of Adolescence*, *10*, 35-43.

Pleak, R., & Meyer-Bahlburg, H. (1990). Sexual behavior and AIDS knowledge of young male prostitutes in Manhattan. *Journal of Sex Research*, *27*(4), 557-587.

Rotheram-Borus, M.J., Rosario, M., Meyer-Bahlburg, H., Koopman, C., Dopkins, S.,

& Davies, M. (1994). Sexual and substance use acts of gay and bisexual male adolescents in New York City. *Journal of Sex Research, 31*(1), 47-57.

Ryan, C., & Futterman, D. (1998). *Lesbian and gay youth: Care and counseling.* New York: Columbia University Press.

Schwartz, W. (1976). Between client and system: Mediating function. In R. Roberts & H. Northern (Eds.), *Theories of social work with groups* (pp. 171-197). New York: Columbia University Press.

Silbert, M. (1980). *Sexual assault and prostitution: Phase one.* Washington, DC: National Institutes of Mental Health.

Van Sant, G. (Director) (1991). *My Own Private Idaho.* [Film].

Practice with Transgendered Youth and Their Families

Ken Cooper

SUMMARY. Each of the ways of being transgendered relates to individuals' sense of themselves as sexed and gendered persons. Finding the 'best fit' in terms of individual and family relations requires being open to and exploring the multiple meanings of sex and gender. For families this can be difficult, confusing and painful. This paper explores a wide range of issues confronting social work practice with transgendered persons and their families. *[Article copies available for a fee from The Haworth Document Delivery Service: 1-800-342-9678. E-mail address: getinfo@haworthpressinc.com <Website: http://www.haworthpressinc.com>]*

KEYWORDS. Transgendered, social work practice with families, gender issues

INTRODUCTION

There is, inevitably, one question that has ushered each of us into family life: Is it a boy or a girl? The question is not asked of us, of course. It is assumed that the answer is simple and apparent. Someone looks at our genitalia and decides. This decision is assumed to be definitive and outside of our power. It will shape much of our future

---

Ken Cooper is a second year MSW student at Hunter College School of Social Work in New York City.

[Haworth co-indexing entry note]: "Practice with Transgendered Youth and Their Families." Cooper, Ken. Co-published simultaneously in *Journal of Gay & Lesbian Social Services* (Harrington Park Press, an imprint of The Haworth Press, Inc.) Vol. 10, No. 3/4, 1999, pp. 111-129; and: *Social Services with Transgendered Youth* (ed: Gerald P. Mallon) Harrington Park Press, an imprint of The Haworth Press, Inc., 1999, pp. 111-129. Single or multiple copies of this article are available for a fee from The Haworth Document Delivery Service [1-800-342-9678, 9:00 a.m. - 5:00 p.m. (EST). E-mail address: getinfo@haworthpressinc.com].

life. Few of us question the assignment that was made at birth. Fewer still question the meaning of the question. Must we be a boy or a girl? Are these the only two options? Are they mutually and clearly distinguishable, or do we have a choice in the matter?

There is probably no aspect of working with the transgendered community that is more striking than the discovery of the range and diversity of human sex and gender. For any individual, whether we identify as transgendered or not, this can be confusing, frightening, intimidating, exhilarating, and difficult. In a world that insists on the duality and consistency of sex and gender, coming to understand transgenderism is a challenge. For transgendered individuals, their families and for social workers, there is little support in understanding and shaping a life that transcends this duality. Social workers often feel as their clients do–adrift in a sea of the changing and seemingly unknowable possibilities. Furthermore they may find little help in understanding these possibilities by examining the literature available to them.

Written from a medical rather than a social perspective, the literature tends to pathologize gender variance and almost exclusively assumes a "transsexual" model. This, unfortunately, can act to limit understanding of the diversity of transgendered lives. While some transgendered individuals desire to "transition" from one sexed body to another by means of hormones, electrolysis and surgery, not all do and fewer still have the economic ability to do so. An increasing number of transgendered individuals are choosing to identify as neither male nor female and are claiming unique contours of sex and gender that offer new and unlimited possibilities. Understanding the nature of these possibilities requires a language that challenges the cultural assumptions of sex and gender. The language and literature of transgendered existence is only now emerging as the transgendered community develops and we begin to think beyond the binary of male and female, man and woman, masculine and feminine (Bornstein, 1994; Feinberg, 1997; Wilchins, 1997).

The term 'transgendered' is a relatively new term that is inclusive of a wide variety of ways that a person might be non-traditionally gendered: intersexed infants, cross-dressers, she-males, he-shes, transsexuals, transvestites, drag queens, gender-blenders, female impersonators, and others (Feinberg, 1997). Each of these ways of being transgendered presents a different set of relationships to individuals' sense of themselves as sexed and gendered persons. Finding the 'best fit' in terms of individual and family relations requires exploring the multiple meanings of sex and gender. The exploration of these options requires not only that we turn inside and unravel complicated feelings about who we are, but that we examine and enter into dialogue with others about how we are perceived.

Sex and gender shape the ways in which we relate to others and how they relate to us. The "father" who reveals his understanding of himself as a woman, or the "daughter" who insists on wearing boys' clothes and being referred to by the pronoun "he," are not simply expressing their innermost sense of self but are re-establishing their relationship to the world. For families this can be difficult, confusing, and painful. When the literature describing the experience of transgendered individuals focuses on individual dysphoria, discomfort, unhappiness and family unrest, it is not surprising that families ask themselves where they went wrong. Social workers working with the families of transgendered individuals often discover that they have entered into a dialogue concerning things they themselves only marginally comprehend. This paper explores social work practice issues with transgendered persons and their families. Exploring some of the myths regarding sex and gender identity will assist the social worker in helping the family understand and adapt to new ways of being along with their transgendered members.

SEX, GENDER, ATTRIBUTES, AND ROLES

It is impossible to understand the gender-variant family member without drawing distinctions between sex and gender, and articulating some of our assumptions about them. Sex refers to the biological status of being a male, female, or intersexed. Because intersexuality is commonly denied by our culture, reference to our sex generally means being either male or female. Gender, on the other hand, refers to the social role we play. Generally this implies a sense of ourselves as a man or a woman. Gender is 'read' by others on the basis of gender attributes that we convey. Although the range of "acceptable" attributes varies from culture to culture, it is generally assumed that masculine attributes appropriately belong to men, and feminine attributes appropriately belong to women. The cult of gender remains so entrenched in our culture that displays of inappropriate gender attributes, such as femininity in men and masculinity in women, are commonly met with violence both inside and outside the family (Mallon, 1998).

In Western culture, it is believed that we were born distinctly male or female and therefore will grow up to be a man or a woman. It is also commonly assumed that it is "natural" that being of one or the other sex leads one to the development of the corresponding gender (i.e., because I was born a male, that I am a boy who will become a man). Our gender training and segregation begins from our earliest days as people respond to us and treat us as a boy or a girl. Even infants are assigned pink or blue blankets based on their assigned gender. Almost every aspect of our lives is shaped, if not determined, by our gender assignment. Demonstrating gender traits or identity that challenge expectations inevitably evokes the reaction that something is wrong with us.

Seeing each other *through* the lenses of gender (Bern, 1993), families tend to assume that they know and understand each member's sex and gender and expect that it will remain consistent with their understandings. But despite these cultural prescriptions, our wider experience tells us that neither sex nor gender are bi-polar, inevitably correlated, and invariant. Helping families to understand and adapt to the transgendered member often requires that the social worker assist them in examining gender–looking *at* the lenses of gender, not simply *through* them (Bern, 1993). There is no telling at what point in the life cycle the individual will come to a transgendered identity and in what unique fashion it will be manifested. Looking at some ways of being transgendered, such as intersexuality in infants, gender variation in children, transsexuality in adolescence and adults, and some new gender options being explored in the transgendered community, may help families understand and grow along with their transgendered member.

INTERSEXUALITY IN INFANTS

At birth we are assigned a gender based on some observation about our sex. In short, this generally means that if the baby has a penis then it is a boy, and if it has a vagina then it is a girl. The presence of a penis or vagina, however, is only one of many biological criteria indicating sex and is not always consistent with other criteria. Hormones, chromosomes, and internal reproductive organs can also act as indicators of sex in the infant. When infants are born with ambiguous or hermaphroditic genitalia (known as virilization), surgery is generally performed to more clearly articulate the child's sex as recognizably male or female because it is assumed that *all* children *must* be either male or female. More than ninety percent of these children are assigned female because medicine cannot reproduce through surgery a fully functioning penis. Current estimates are that 1.7 out of every 1,000 births show ambiguous or hermaphroditic sex characteristics (Intersex Society of North America, 1996). For most of these children, their intersexed past is hidden from them, resulting in feelings of confusion and maladjustment as they grow older.

An increasing number of female-to-male identified transgendered individuals are discovering that they were assigned the sex of female as a result of ambiguous sex characteristics at birth, as the following case illustrates. Max was raised as a female from birth and came out as a lesbian while in college (Boenke, 1999). Although Max was female identified at the time, "she" knew that when she was born the doctors could not tell if she was a boy or a girl and had performed surgery that had left her with a vagina that was scarred and painful. She knew her body was different from other women's bodies and felt that she couldn't hide it, yet didn't know how lesbian women would respond to her intersexed status.

As an adult, sexual activity for Max was difficult and painful both physically and emotionally. During her college years she became involved with another woman and together they set out to understand her intersexed body. During the four months that they spent examining her infant medical records, Max began questioning her female sexual assignment and battled unwavering depression and suicidal ideation. Finally, she and her lover began attending support groups for intersexed individuals. There they met other people like Max and began to break down some of their stereotypes and expectations regarding Max's female body and lesbian identity. Max has now begun the process of transitioning to a male identified gender role and now feels a greater sense of control over his life.

Although only a small percentage of adults who will later identify as transgendered are intersexed at birth, it is an important field of research for two reasons. First, it underscores our cultural bias towards understanding sex and gender as an irrefutable binary, and second, it is the first arena where parents will be asked to interfere with the natural basis of sex and gender in their children. Dr. Ann Fausto-Sterling

(1993, p. 131) has argued that rather than the two sexes we believe to exist, "there are many gradations running from female to male; and depending on how one calls the shots, one can argue that along the spectrum lie at least five sexes–and perhaps even more."

In recent years the Intersex Society of North America (ISNA) has evolved to help intersexed individuals and their parents understand and cope with the experience of being sexed in a way that is largely misunderstood in our society. In the past, infant genital surgery has been the assumed treatment for intersexed children, but ISNA has begun to question the wisdom of that prescription. Their position is that parents need to be informed that in most cases there is no evidence that infant genital surgery is either necessary or beneficial and that there is significant evidence that it may result in pain, depression, suicidal feelings, and social or sexual dysfunction. Many intersexed individuals argue that genital surgery should be postponed until children are old enough to make decisions for themselves. Encouraging parents to raise an intersexed child is of course very difficult, given the lack of support and understanding currently evident in society. Intersexed individuals need protection, support, and understanding. Only with truthful information about their intersexed children can parents begin to advocate for their children's needs in schools and other settings.

GENDER VARIATION IN CHILDREN

Every aspect of our lives is permeated with situations where we are asked to identify our gender. Purchasing clothing or toys and even the ability to stand while urinating are controlled by signs and forms that demand a choice: Are you a boy or are you a girl? It is often difficult for family members to comprehend and support the transgendered individual because we lack the language to discuss the complexities and varieties of ways of being sexed and gendered.

Gender identity develops in children by the age of three, when most identify themselves as either boys or girls. Because it is popularly assumed that there is a "natural" relationship between sex and gender, children who question their birth assignment are pathologized and labeled "gender dysphoric."

Experience tells us that there is not always a correlation between sex and gender identity, and anthropological studies indicate that numerous cultures allow for a wide variety of gender-variant identities and social roles (Denny, 1997; Williams, 1986). Nonetheless, families may often feel confused, angry or guilty when a child or adolescent demonstrates transgendered behavior or identity. Furthermore, due to misinformation and a lack of education regarding sex and gender options, transgendered people and their families may mistakenly be advised that treatment for "gender identity disorder" is their only option in dealing with the discomforts of raising a non-traditionally gendered child. Gender identity, according to the American Psychological Association (1980), is the sense of "knowing" what one's gender is, and gender role is the public expression of that identity. Coming to the understanding that one's birth gender assignment is wrong is difficult enough for any individual. The American Pyschiatric Association's (1994) belief that gender 'dysphoria' is an illness complicates this process for gender variant children and their families. Parents will unfortunately be surrounded by social pressure and professional advice that insists that something is wrong with their child.

Childhood is undoubtedly a difficult period for gender variant children and their parents. There is virtually no social support in any of our institutions for the gender variant child, and the parent who attempts to negotiate accommodations for the child will undoubtedly meet with misunderstanding, incredulity and resistance. In such an environment, it is easy to blame the child for his or her failure to adapt to gender norms. Often the child will respond with depression, anxiety, fear, anger, low self-esteem, self-mutilation, and suicidal ideation. Unfortunately, this is often taken as further evidence that something is wrong with the child. Rather than focus on the systems that will not allow these children to develop in their own way, treatment usually focuses on the children's "maladaptive" gender identity.

"Gender Identity Disorder" (GID) first appeared in the American Psychiatric Association's Diagnostic and Statistical Manual III (DSM-III) in 1980. GID is described as an "incongruence between assigned sex (i.e., the sex that is recorded on the birth certificate) and gender identity." The DSM-III goes on to describe a broad range of gender variant behaviors that may be observed in individuals, and insists that "in the vast majority of cases the onset of the disorder can be traced back to childhood." GID is considered a disorder even though "some of these children, particularly girls, show no other signs of psychopathology" (American Psychiatric Association, 1980).

The introduction of GID in children into the DSM came as the result of a United States Government-funded experiment on gender variant boys that took place in the 1970s. These studies found that very few "feminine" boys will go on to become transsexuals, but that a high percentage of them (one half to two thirds) will become homosexual (Burke, 1996). GID was added to the DSM-III in 1980 following the removal of homosexuality as an illness from that volume (Bern, 1993). Treatment, which is justified in the name of preventing transsexualism, focuses instead on modifying gender variant behavior and may all too easily be used to "treat" future homosexuality.

Pauline Parks (1998), a transgender activist, argues that every psychiatrist who diagnoses GID in a patient merely by virtue of his/her transgender identity is complicit in the manipulation and control of transgendered people and their bodies, and in diagnosing someone with an 'illness' that s/he does not have, engages in behavior which is not only unethical, but which constitutes medical malpractice. Children are particularly vulnerable to suffering medical injustices in the name of treating gender identity disorder. Social workers can provide parents with a broader focus and expertise than might be provided by other helping professionals.

Given the level of medical, cultural, and social misunderstanding that gender variant children will endure it is not surprising that many will develop social isolation, depression, and self-esteem problems. Children who are diagnosed with GID are often treated with brutal aversion therapies intended to adjust their gender orientation (Burke, 1996; Scholinsky, 1997). Social workers should assist parents in resisting these treatments. Treatment for depression and associated conditions should not attempt to enforce gender stereotypical behavior.

TRANSSEXUALITY

Often transsexuality is the only framework families have for understanding transgendered lives. When Christine Jorgenson went to Denmark in 1952 for her sex-change operation, she became the first internationally famous transsexual. Her case, which was widely covered by the media, popularized the notion of transsexuals as being "trapped inside the wrong body," and suggested a hormonal and surgical solution to an "aberrant" condition that was causing the transsexual individual great psychological pain. In 1966, Dr. Harry Benjamin published "The Transsexual Phenomenon" which did a great deal to heighten awareness of transsexuals and to underscore that it was a female as well as a male phenomenon. Nonetheless, Dr. Benjamin's book still emphasized transsexualism as an aberration or illness. Characteristic of transsexualism is the desire to alter the body through hormones and surgery to more appropriately match the individual's gender identity. Because we live in a world that assumes 'man' or 'woman' to be our only choices, this kind of surgery is often designated as "Sex Reassignment Surgery." Contemporary transgender activists have suggested that "Genital Reconstruction Surgery" is a more accurate description because it more precisely describes the nature of the intervention.

Individuals seeking sex reassignment enter into a complicated relationship with the medical and psychiatric establishments which act as 'gatekeepers' to the medical procedures. Dr. Benjamin's institute developed the Standards of Care (SOC) that are used to determine the appropriateness of an individual's desire for sex reassignment surgery, and that provide controls to insure that individuals do not rush into surgery that they may later regret. Coming to the decision to seek hormonal and surgical body alteration is indeed a difficult decision. Rather than simplifying the process, the medicalization of transsexuality often complicates this decision. The medicalized and pathologized notion of transsexuals pre-supposes that one must be very uncomfortable with one's body in order to seek out sex reassignment surgery so that one is in fact "rewarded" for their psychological pain and discomfort. Many transsexuals fear that if they do not register the appropriate amount of discomfort with their bodies they will not be approved for surgery. This acts to reinforce notions of transsexuality as an illness that has a medical and surgical treatment.

Sex reassignment surgery may be a difficult topic for families to talk about. Literature which is intended to inform them may frighten them by pathologizing the transsexual individual. Social workers can help families by normalizing and reframing the desire of transsexuals to alter their bodies. Wendy Chapkis (1986) has suggested that we all alter our bodies to more accurately match our gender identities.

> . . . nearly everyone attempts to reshape their anatomy to bring it more comfortably close to the sex and gender ideal. Most women shave their legs and underarms because it is not only unfeminine,

it is somehow unfemale to be hairy. The moustached woman will almost certainly contemplate a change of anatomy through depilatories or electrolysis to avoid being addressed as "sir," to rid herself of the confusing sensation of stubble, to ease the mixed signals. A small chested woman may receive breast implants to help her feel more womanly. A short man may wear elevator shoes and a small man devote himself to body building to create a more "manly" physique. All are trying to fix a conflict between social and sexual identity and anatomical reality. (Chapkis, 1986, p. 155)

What transsexuals do to alter their bodily appearance, according to Sandra Lipsitz Bern (1993), is only different in degree (and direction) from what "normal" people do to match their bodies to their gender identities. By helping families understand how we all create gender through manipulation of our bodies, our clothing, and the gender clues we convey, we also help them accept and accommodate the transgendered member. The choice to alter one's body can and should be framed as an act of empowerment over one's life, rather than as a surgical solution to an uncomfortable situation.

Parents may often find themselves facing questions of transsexual identity during the child's adolescent years. Often the onset of puberty will bring about a feeling of crisis in transgendered individuals because they find their bodies changing in ways that do not match their gender identities. Transgendered teens may feel betrayed, isolated, shameful, and bewildered by the changes occurring in their bodies. These feelings may be accompanied by a sense of panic and immediacy that these changes must be stopped. Transgendered teenagers will often feel confused about their sexual orientation, and are frequently subject to harassment and humiliation by their peers and by adults.

It is often during these discomfiting years that transsexuals will begin contemplating sex reassignment surgery and will often express frustration at their lack of access to immediate treatment. Support groups where they can share these frustrations and explore ways of coping can be extremely helpful at this time. Because most teens will have a complete absence of transsexual role models, it is particularly desirable that transsexual teens have access to individuals who have gone through the surgical procedures who can help put perspective on the process for them. Support groups can help transgendered individuals sort through their feelings about their sex and gender and help them in coming to an understanding of themselves in relation to transgenderism and transsexuality.

Jaleeka is a 15-year-old Dominican male to female transsexual, living in New York City. While she is too young to begin hormones and too poor to consider surgery, she is quite certain that she will begin the transition as soon as she can legally do so. Before meeting other transsexuals, Jaleeka was perceived as a young gay male and she was depressed, suicidal, and in conflict with her family, for whom homosexuality was not considered a viable option. Jaleeka knew that she had always thought of herself as a girl but she had never met another transsexual. When she first learned of transsexuality, she came to see herself as a "straight" woman who needed surgery in order to have the body she desired. She grew her hair, began dressing in woman's clothes on a full time basis and assumed a girl's role in the family. For her family, this transition was easier and more understandable than accepting an effeminate, homosexual son.

Social workers should be cautious in supporting transsexuality as an alternative to homosexuality. Nonetheless, a supportive and non-judgmental environment may help transsexual teenagers come to terms with their gender identity. Not only did Jaleeka benefit from support groups where she met transsexuals who had been through sex reassignment surgery, but her parents benefited enormously both from contact with post-operative transsexuals and their parents.

Even those individuals who are interested in sex reassignment surgery will find it difficult to obtain. Most insurance companies explicitly exclude hormone therapy and sex reassignment surgery. Furthermore, this is a highly regulated medical industry whose benefits may or may not be awarded to an individual depending on the recommendation of a so-called 'gender specialist.' Often gender specialists are just the opposite of what the term implies, offering little perspective on the way gender operates in society and distilling options down to "passing" as the "opposite" gender. Many transgendered individuals find themselves poorly understood by these 'gender specialists.'

There is a growing number of people who are diagnosed as gender dysphoric, but for one reason or another are not deemed good candidates for sex reassignment. Gender identity programs can turn down applicants for many reasons–age, a history of psychiatric illnesses, homosexuality, fetishism, sadomasochism, a criminal record, inability to tolerate hormones, a medical history of cancer, possessing a face or body that the surgeon believes will never pass muster as a member of the gender preference ("somatically inappropriate"), poverty, employment in the sex industry, a refusal to aspire to be a feminine woman or a masculine male, or uppitiness. (Califia, 1997, p. 169)

Whether by choice or by circumstance, increasing numbers of transgendered people are discovering that 'transitioning' is not an option for them. There has been an increasing awareness of individuals who reject the notion that one must 'transition' and 'pass' as the opposite gender in order to fit into the binary gender system. Growing awareness of the range of gender options between male and female has revolutionized transgender politics and increased gender options available to us.

NEW GENDER OPTIONS

Although the advent of sex reassignment surgery in the 1950s offered new possibilities for gender variant individuals, it also solidified an understanding of transgenderism that fed rather than dispelled some myths regarding sex and gender. It did little to dispel the notion that the binary gender system was a natural phenomenon. It ignored the possibility that an individual might have a healthy relationship to their transgendered status, or that there might be a wide variety of ways of being sexed and/or gendered that may or may not include body alteration.

Increasingly, transgendered individuals are coming to understand their lives as outside of the sex and gender binary and are discovering that this understanding increases the options available to them. Some choose not to undergo bodily transformation, but to dress and live their lives in differently gendered roles. Cross-dressers or male-bodied women, for example, may inhabit a male body but live dressed and in the social role of women. Gender-blenders may incorporate physical and cultural characteristics of both genders in a way that feels comfortable and appropriate to them. Many transgendered people have discovered that some forms of body modification such as breast removal, or hormone therapy may result in just the right amount of male or female characteristics but may not choose to undergo genital reconstruction surgery. Gender-blenders, she-males, or he-shes are representative of this kind of sex and gender mix. 'Transvestite' has traditionally been a term for individuals who maintain their original sex and gender identities but attain sexual gratification from dressing in the clothing of the opposite sex, but today the term may refer to individuals who prefer the clothing of the "opposite" sex for any of a variety of reasons. New sex and gender variations are being discovered or invented each day by individuals who are exploring their unique needs.

The understanding that we do not need to trade one gender for another but can find or invent a mix that is just right for us has revolutionized the possibilities for transgendered living. New gender possibilities will increase the need for adaptations within the family because of the way these gender possibilities confront our 'knowledge' of sex and gender as a binary system. It should not matter to the social worker whether the transgendered individual decides to be male, female, or somewhere in the middle. However, in helping families work through the difficulties of transition, we can encourage new forms of relationships that will support change and maximize freedom of choice.

FAMILY TRANSITIONS

Coming to understand a family member's transgendered identity is a difficult and confusing experience. The nature or our relationship with a son, daughter, wife, husband, mother, father, sister, brother, aunt, or uncle is intricately woven into what we believe we know about the consistency of gender. Learning to reframe a relationship with the family member who has begun to question or redefine his or her gender status may result in difficult and confusing alterations in the structure of the family. Understanding and accommodating these changes in family relationships is difficult at best and often family members experience the same confusion, guilt, anger, pain, and disappointment that the transgendered family member has already struggled with. Family members need time to grieve the loss of a relationship as they understood it, and they need support and education in building a new relationship based on an unfamiliar gender dynamic (Brown & Rounsley, 1996; Lesser, 1999). Social workers may help the families of transgendered individuals by encouraging them to explore the meaning of gender in their relationships. They must also be prepared to deal with a family's guilt, embarrassment, and shame about having a transgendered family member.

Families may find it difficult to adjust to the use of new pronouns, or the use of a new name for a family member. But for many this is the first step in altering the terms of a relationship. The person who was a "son" may feel strongly that his parents refer to her as their "daughter." Family members who forget and use the wrong pronoun may discover that they have caused pain without intending to do so. Whatever the circumstances, social workers should not underestimate the transition that is required from family members in adapting to a new relationship. The mother of a "heterosexual son" who must come to grips with the fact that she now has a "lesbian daughter" may feel betrayed by her own child. Alternatively, family members may accept the newly gendered member without altering some basic terms of the relationship. Christine Howey, for example, is a playwright whose father has transitioned to female. Christine now refers to her father as a woman and uses the pronoun "she" when speaking of her. Nonetheless, Christine still recognizes this woman as her father. The terms of new relationships will have to be negotiated within the family. Adjusting to new gender relationships takes time. Social workers can provide support by offering reassurance to all family members that this transition can happen.

FORMING FAMILIES

Transgendered individuals will, of course, form relationships and families of their own. Forming relationships requires honesty, acceptance, and understanding. Nonetheless, many professionals have encouraged their clients to hide their transsexuality and "pass" as their new gender. Gender clinics have even encouraged transsexuals to make up life histories that would validate their new gender identity. Transsexualism, as Kate Bornstein (1994) points out, is the only condition for which the recommended therapy is to lie.

> When I was growing up, people who lived cross-gendered lives were pressured into hiding deep within the darkest closets they could find. Those who came out of their closets were either

studied under a microscope, ridiculed in the tabloids, or made exotic in porn books, so it paid to hide. It paid to lie. That was probably the most painful part of it: the lying to friends and family and lovers, the pretending to be someone I wasn't. (Bornstein, 1994, p. 177)

The perpetuation of this perspective made dating and romance difficult, if not impossible, for many transgendered individuals. As transgendered individuals develop a broader, healthier, and more honest understanding of the meaning of their lives, they discover the need for partners who understand and are supportive of their transgendered bodies.

Much of the literature about transgendered people in relationships has focused on the difficulties: wives in turmoil when their husbands come out to them as cross-dressers, or transsexuals who fear being "discovered" by their lovers. However, as the transgendered community grows in self-awareness, new bodies of literature are emerging that speak to successful and honest relationships between transgendered people and their partners (Boenke, 1999; Califia, 1997). Often, these relationships must transcend the gender-based sexual orientation of our culture. The wife who comes to accept her husband as a woman, or the lesbian whose partner transitions to male may find that their relationship and sexual orientation can no longer be contained by the categories of 'gay' or 'straight.' Pat Califia (1997) has suggested that there is a broad range of individuals who may prefer some form of transgenderism in their partners and that this group may be a sexual minority in their own right. For many, involvement with a transgendered partner may offer an edge of excitement and discovery in both the social and sexual arena that may draw them to these partners.

Increasingly, transgendered individuals are beginning to form primary relationships with each other. These relationships, which transcend contemporary notions of hetero- and homosexuality, may open doors for all of us in contemplating other ways in which our sexuality may be organized besides gender. Sylvia Riviera is a female identified drag queen who played an important role in the Stonewall Rebellions. While she has always been attracted to men, she recently has found herself in a relationship with a male-to-female transsexual. This relationship surprised her and, because she is legally still a man and her partner is legally a woman, they are planning a wedding. "I never thought that I was going to get into the situation of marrying some-body, but I'm very happy. I don't plan on getting a sex change as my partner has already done. But I feel that both of us being transgend-ered, we understand what the other has gone through . . . we just want to be ourselves. And she's a great person for me" (Riviera, 1999, p. 49).

BUILDING COMMUNITY, BUILDING FAMILY

How we define the family is vital because, as Hartman and Laird (1983) have pointed out, it is in defining the family that we define what models and social policies are stimulated and endorsed, for what families social policies are developed, and "even more basically . . . who is considered 'normal' and who is labeled 'deviant.'" The family should be, of course, a source of support, nourishment, and stability for each of its members. Given the wide variation in human circum-stance, it naturally follows that family would take on a wide variety of forms. The strength of the family resides in its function rather than its form. Nonetheless, as a culture, we frequently fret about what has become of 'the family' and much public discussion of 'the family' focuses on a rather narrow structural view of what constitutes family. The family occupies a prominent place in our public discourse and, as Hartman and Laird (1983) point out, it is one topic that "sends people running to their philosophical battle stations."

In 1996, the Congress passed almost unanimously and President Clinton unhesitatingly signed the "Defense of Marriage Act" (D.O.M.A.). This act, which was hastily thrown together and pushed through Congress by "pro-family" forces that felt threatened by the growing recognition of same-sex unions, defines marriage as strictly between "one man" and "one woman." The intention of the law is clear–that there should be governmental recognition of only one form of family. The ease with which the Defense of Marriage Act was passed underscores that it is not just the religious right wing that is vested in limiting options in forming families, but that the conservative political agenda of so-called 'family values' is a potent, mainstream dogma. The Defense of Marriage Act has no interest in supporting families but in maintaining a narrow definition of the family. D.O.M.A. rewards and reinforces participation in a bi-polar, heterocentric family structure.

It is perhaps an indication of the invisibility of transgendered people that the crafters of D.O.M.A. did not deem it necessary to define a "man" and a "woman." This means that transgendered individuals often find themselves in unusual (and even sometimes advantageous) circumstances in relation to the law. In some states, birth certificates are relied upon to assure that partners seeking a marriage license are "one man and one woman." This loophole has allowed for the marriage of a gay male couple where one partner is a FTM transsexual (Boenke, 1999). Mitch is a female to male transsexual who is attracted to other men. When he and his partner applied for a marriage license they were told that only gender mixed couples were granted licenses and that birth certificates were necessary to prove gender. While Mitch had legally changed his drivers license from female to male, state law did not allow changes in birth certificates. He was therefore able to produce a birth certificate that showed that he was a woman, and he and his partner were granted a marriage license. They may be the only gay male couple legally married in America.

Limiting the ways in which we think about and define family constrains our ability to create family. As transgendered people grow into new relationships with the very idea of gender, many discover that the traditional family is no longer a safe or supportive place for them. This, however, does not decrease their needs for belongingness, intimacy, interpersonal connectedness, and all of the day-to-day resources that belonging to a family has to offer. Transgendered persons, who wish to live fully their transgendered identity, need forms of family that will support and nourish their existence. Families provide economic support and interdependence, foster a sense of emotional connectivity, stability and belongingness, help develop our capacity for intimacy, and provide for a sense of generativity (Hartman & Laird, 1983). The function and benefits of family are evident in differing degrees in a wide variety of social structures available to us. Recognition and reinforcement of structures that provide for the needs of transgendered individuals may result in new and more communal forms of family.

In the film *Paris Is Burning* (Livingston, 1991), which focuses on young transgendered inner-city kids who participate in the Harlem Drag Ball culture, it is the 'house' that provides an alternative to their often dysfunctional families. Each 'house' has a 'mother,' someone of legendary status in the Drag Ball scene, who helps her 'children' in finding their own way through the culture. The children take the mother's name as their own, a symbol of their strong identification with the house to which they belong. The film portrays the ways in which the house culture provides them with intimacy, understanding, support, and a sense of belongingness as they struggle with their emerging gender identity and the many questions that it raises in their lives. Not enough studies have examined the usefulness of alternative family structures in the transgendered community and further studies of the house culture in particular may provide wider understanding of ways in which family function may be served in the lives of otherwise marginalized individuals.

The growing transgendered movement may be invaluable in helping transgendered individuals redefine themselves in relation to gender, family, and larger social structures. Lombardi (1999) has found that involvement in transgender organizations resulted in a strengthening of the individual's identity and an increase in activities outside of club meetings as well. For individuals who have been told that they are 'sick' and must hide their transgendered status, these social structures provide support, encouragement, education, and understanding. Transgender social networks empower transgendered individuals to free themselves from the control of the medical establishment and establish new forms of relationships and families that support them and their transgendered identities. They create a hospitable niche for transgendered individuals where they can begin to explore the nature of their transgendered lives, and find meaning in new relationships that may not fit the traditional definitions of family. Family is too important to be narrowly defined by blood, kinship, or legal parameters. In building community and reaching out to others, transgendered people are actively creating family in ways that support, encourage, and celebrate transgendered lives.

REFERENCES

American Psychiatric Association. (1980). *Diagnostic and statistical manual of mental disorders* (3rd ed.). Washington, DC: Author.
American Psychiatic Association. (1994). *Diagnostic and statistical manual of mental disorders* (4th ed.). Washington, DC: Author.
Benjamin, H. (1966). *The transsexual phenomenon.* New York: Julian Press.
Bern, S. L. (1993). *The lenses of gender.* New Haven: Yale University Press.
Boenke, M. (1999). *Trans forming families: Real stories about transgendered loved ones.* Imperial Beach: Walter Trook Publishing.

Bornstein, K. (1994). *Gender outlaw: On men, women and the rest of us.* New York: Vintage Books.

Brown, M., & Rounsley, C.A. (1996) *True selves: Understanding transsexualism for family, friends, co-workers and helping professionals.* San Francisco: Jossey Bass.

Burke, P. (1996). *Gender shock: Exploding the myths of male and female.* NY: Bantam Books.

Califia, P. (1997). *Sex changes: The politics of transgenderism.* San Francisco: Cleis Press.

Chapkis, W. (1986). *Beauty secrets: Women and the politics of appearance.* Boston: South End Press.

Denny, D. (1997) Transgender: Some historical, cross-cultural and contemporary models and methods for coping and treatment. In B. Bullough, V. Bullough, & J. Elias (Eds.). *Gender blending* (pp. 102-113). Amherst, NY: Prometheus Books.

Fausto-Sterling, A. (1993, March-April). The five sexes: Why male and female are not enough. *The Sciences,* 20-25.

Feinberg, L. (1997). *Transgender warriors: Making history from Joan of Arc to Dennis Rodman.* Boston: Beacon Press.

Hartman, A., & Laird, J. (1983). *Family centered social work.* New York: Free Press.

Intersex Society of North America. (1996). Intersexuality–Frequently asked questions. World Wide Web: www.sexuality.org/l/transgen/intefaq.html.

Lesser, J.G. (1999). When your son becomes your daughter: A mother's adjustment to a transgender child. *Families in Society,* 41-51.

Livingston, J. (Director) (1991). *Paris Is Burning.*

Lombardi, E.L. (1999). Integration within a transgender social network and its effects on members' social and political activity. *Journal of Homosexuality, 37*(1), 109-126.

Mallon, G.P. (1998). Practice with gay and lesbian families. In G.P. Mallon (Ed.), *Foudations of social work practice with lesbian and gay persons.* Binghamton, NY: The Haworth Press, Inc.

Riviera, S. (1999, June 27). I never thought I was going to be a part of gay history. *New York Times Magazine,* p. 49.

Scholinsky, D. (1997). *The last time I wore a dress.* New York: Riverhead Books.

Wilchins, R.A. (1997). *Read my lips: Sexual subversion and the end of gender.* Firebrand.

Williams, W. (1986). *The spirit and the flesh: Sexual diversity in American Indian culture.* Boston: Beacon Press.

A Call for Organizational Trans-Formation

Gerald P. Mallon

SUMMARY. In the collection of papers presented in this volume, several authors have enumerated the needs of transgendered youth and identified the obstacles that youth-serving agencies face in addressing their needs. This final paper, using case examples from several nationally-known transgendered affirming agencies, offers recommendations on agency philosophies concerning the reality of transgendered youth and additionally offers suggestions on ways to create safe, welcoming, and nurturing environments. *[Article copies available for a fee from The Haworth Document Delivery Service: 1-800-342-9678. E-mail address: getinfo@haworthpressinc.com <Website: http://www.haworthpressinc.com>]*

KEYWORDS. Organizational change, transgendered, transformation, agency-based practice

INTRODUCTION

The dilemmas faced by transgendered youth and their families are clear (Feinberg, 1993; Israel & Tarver, 1997; Scholinski, 1997). Youth-serving agencies, already challenged by many substantial issues, tend to exhibit a range of sensitivities to transgendered youth. At one extreme, some agencies openly discriminate against transgendered

---

Gerald P. Mallon, DSW, is Assistant Professor, Hunter College School of Social Work, New York City, NY.

[Haworth co-indexing entry note]: "A Call for Organizational Trans-Formation." Mallon, Gerald P. Co-published simultaneously in *Journal of Gay & Lesbian Social Services* (Harrington Park Press, an imprint of The Haworth Press, Inc.) Vol. 10, No. 3/4, 1999, pp. 131-142; and: *Social Services with Transgendered Youth* (ed: Gerald P. Mallon) Harrington Park Press, an imprint of The Haworth Press, Inc., 1999, pp. 131-142. Single or multiple copies of this article are available for a fee from The Haworth Document Delivery Service [1-800-342-9678, 9:00 a.m. - 5:00 p.m. (EST). E-mail address: getinfo@haworthpressinc.com].

youth. At the other extremity, there are those which are affirming in their approaches and strongly advocate for their needs. Most youth-serving agencies fall somewhere in the middle. Some youth-serving agencies initiate good faith efforts to become more affirming, but this usually occurs when they come across their first openly transgendered youth. In many cases, such efforts are initiated because the transgendered youth is seen as a "problem." Unfortunately, a more proactive stance, in preparing for working with diverse groups of youth rarely takes place without a precipitating incident.

Youth-serving agencies come into contact with transgendered youth for many of the same reasons that they see other youth: family conflict, health or mental health of the youth, school problems, or the need for an out-of-home placement. The scope of these issues with respect to a transgendered identity requires that all youth-serving agencies become knowledgeable about and sensitive to the needs of transgendered youth. The vulnerability of transgendered youth, particularly at times when they come to the attention of youth-serving agencies, is yet another reason that youth providers should be prepared for working with this population. The most inopportune time to increase one's knowledge about a service population is to learn when they arrive at the agency in a crisis and are in need of immediate assistance.

Case # 1

Green Chimneys Children's Services, initially designed to meet the needs of groups of heterosexually-oriented children and youth aging out of foster care toward independence, is an excellent example of a mainstream child welfare agency that has been transformed into a gay, lesbian, and transgendered affirming organization. Established in New York City in 1947, Green Chimneys Children's Services was conceived, designed and administered by heterosexually-oriented professionals. The agency received financing from private sources to fund their efforts; however, public monies were also a major source of support for all of their programs.

In 1987, however, due in large part to the hiring of an openly gay Associate Executive Director, Green Chimneys Children's Services took a bold step out of the child welfare closet and moved forward by reaching out to provide leadership in child welfare for another unique and underserved population–gay, lesbian, bisexual, transgendered, and questioning (GLBTQ) children, youth, and families affected by issues of sexual orientation. Gay, lesbian, and transgendered professionals were comfortable in working with GLBTQ adolescents, and began to openly address issues, challenge heterocentric policies, and design programs that insured a better fit for gay and lesbian young people and their families. With this new influx of GLBTQ identified staff, the agency's culture, previously heterosexually-oriented, began a process of transformation as the staff openly embraced GLBTQ adolescents into their array of diversity.

In reflecting on this transformational process, one professional from that program made these observations:

> We just decided that we had gay kids and that we did good work with them and we would continue to provide care for them. We made a conscious decision not to discriminate. Initially, we were referred and accepted a number of self-identified gay kids; their orientation was not the issue; their needs fit the mission of the program and they were accepted. Then we began to earn a reputation for being an agency which would take gay kids and then we started to get calls for every gay kid that came through the system. I think at certain points in time the agency was uncomfortable about being stigmatized as "the gay agency" but for the most part they have been very supportive of our efforts. Our openness to accepting gay kids unfortunately has not been the norm. (Mallon, 1998, pp. 101-102)

In taking such a bold step out of the child welfare closet and moving forward to respond to the needs of GLBTQ youth and families, Green Chimneys has had to participate in a major shift in its organizational culture. Green Chimneys Children's Services was the first mainstream child welfare agency in the United States to openly address and respond to the needs and to work toward developing program options that would provide a continuum of care for GLBTQ children, youth, and their families. The organization's administration provided leadership, but the transformation was not always painless.

Green Chimneys and Gay and Lesbian Adolescent Social Services (GLASS), a similar agency in Southern California, have both struggled with being more closely monitored in very different ways by state authorities. Such close scrutiny can be stressful to the operation of a program, but also to program staff who may feel that they are under constant watch. This is, unfortunately, a very real consequence of developing GLBTQ affirming programs. Additionally, not all agency staff were affirming or accepting at first. Religious and cultural biases played a large role in their level of discomfort. A major commitment to on-going training for all levels of staff and maintaining the stance that Green Chimneys has always served youth and families who were most needy, helped to change the organization's culture.

Even though a transgendered youth might still raise an eyebrow if he or she attends a function on Green Chimney's main campus–such youth are always treated with dignity and respect by the staff and residents. Staff in all program areas are aware of the agency's commitment to GLBTQ youth and affected families, and although not all staff fully comprehend the needs of these youth, the New York City branch of the agency continues to educate them and help them move toward acceptance.

In transforming themselves from heterocentric institutions to inclusive environments which affirm and recognize the uniqueness of GLBTQ adolescents, agencies like Green Chimneys had to confront the heterocentrism and strict requirements of gender conformity in their conceptions of GLBTQ youth. Such a transformation entails a process of discernment in scrutinizing their own organizational functions, in examining their boards and policy-making bodies, in reviewing the openness of their staff members toward issues of gender and sexual orientation, and in evaluating their relationship to the GLBTQ communities.

Creating an Affirming Culture

Efforts to increase sensitivity to transgendered youth cannot be sustained in an environment that does not explicitly encourage such undertakings. As agencies struggle to demonstrate their commitment to diversity, they must also be willing to include sexual orientation in that diversity continuum. In doing so, they begin the work necessary for creating a safe and welcoming environment for *all* clients, not just transgendered youth. Once this orientation is set, and the organization's culture shifts to clearly include transgendered concerns, it becomes possible for youth workers to learn about, advocate for, and provide affirming services to transgendered youth (see Gonsiorek, 1982).

Although it is a reality that some agency administrators and Board members might object to transgendered sensitivity awareness or programs specifically geared toward this population, few should take exception to overall approaches designed to increase worker competence in working with clients who are underserved. Inherent in all change efforts are the realities of the political consequences of the change efforts (Frost & Egri, 1991). Such changes can also be viewed as new opportunities for the organization (Dutton, 1992). Organizational paradigm shifts, such as those suggested here, can in the long run, offer more effective services for children, youth, and families in need (Sawyer & Woodlock, 1995).

TRANSFORMING THE ORGANIZATION'S CULTURE

Transformation is a powerful word, but nothing less is needed to create programs that are responsive to the needs of transgendered youth. Appreciation of diversity and a knowledge of the organization's idiosyncratic culture (Kets de Vries & Miller, 1984) are key elements in this process. The examination of an organization's commitment to diversity is a common theme for all youth-serving agency administrators. Diversity approaches in organizations have utilized various components to increase worker competence in meeting the needs of a varied client population, including: in-service training, nondiscrimination policies, participating in culturally specific celebrations, advocacy, client/staff groups that explore diversity, and efforts which encourage a climate that welcomes all people. A transgendered approach could be integrated into any one of these areas. A community-based youth center commemorating Latino History month with a pot-luck dinner representing dishes from various Latino countries, could just as easily celebrate Pride month by inviting a speaker to discuss the events that led to the civil rights struggle for transgendered persons.

Youth oriented agencies must also be committed to creating a safe environment for all youth. The enactment of a zero tolerance policy for violence, weapons, emotional maltreatment, slurs of all types, and direct or indirect mistreatment, conveys to all clients that their safety is a priority. A hearty stance against violence of all types, including verbal harassment, sends an important message to all youth. It says we will try to protect you and you will not be blamed for being yourself. Those who offend are the ones who will be dealt with, because their behavior is unjustified.

All youth benefit from youth workers who are open, honest, and genuine. Everyone benefits from philosophies that indicate an agency's willingness to address difficult issues head on. Giving clients and staff permission to raise controversial topics signals that all people associated with the agency will be treated with respect and dignity.

It is only through intentional and deliberate organizational cultural shifts–true transformation, that a climate supportive of transgendered youth can be developed (Shorr, 1988). Several agencies across the U.S. and in Canada have been successful in creating organizations where transgendered youth are welcomed, feel safe, and have their needs met. Such organizational transformation does not take huge amounts of money, tremendous time commitments on the part of staff, or other expensive overtures. It does, however, take commitment from Board members, Administrators, and other key organizational players, including youth and their families.

Although mainstream youth-serving agencies can be transformed into trans-affirming agencies, in many cases, out of necessity, GLBTQ persons have designed their own agencies to meet the needs of their own communities. The following is an organizational case example of one such agency in Los Angeles.

Case # 2

Despite the fact that in 1979, Governor Jerry Brown had signed an Executive Order preventing social services agencies from denying services to gay, lesbian, bisexual, transgendered, and questioning (GLBTQ) youth, youth serving agencies in California still searched for the next five years for any way that they could effectively serve these youth. Their answer appeared in 1984, when Teresa DeCrescenzo, whose career as a social worker and probation officer gave her a first-hand experience of the poor fit which most GLBTQ young people endured in mainstream and publicly-funded child welfare agencies, founded the GLASS program. In 1985, shortly after incorporation as a city, West Hollywood City Council voted to grant GLASS start-up funding in the amount of $55,000 to set up a six-bed licensed group home. Financing was difficult, some in the community responded negatively at election time, and politicians who originally supported the effort came under fire for their support. But the neonate agency survived.

By 1987, with the demand for child welfare placements increasing, the Los Angeles County Department of Probation asked the organization to open a second facility with a grant of $45,000. By this point, GLASS had already developed a solid reputation in the community. At the same time, the agency responded to the call to provide effective residential programming for HIV-infected youth. At the time when this subgroup was added to the organization's mission statement, HIV was seen as a gay disease. At present, the majority of HIV-positive youth living in GLASS programs are heterosexual (Greeley, 1994).

In 1989, the agency expanded its mission to include foster care and initiated a program which recruited, screened, trained, certified, and supervised foster parents. Although this agency's specific mission is to provide care for gay and lesbian adolescents in five group homes and in 135 foster homes, they do not discriminate against heterosexually-oriented young people who live in the Los Angeles area. The agency employs GLBTQ and heterosexually-oriented staff with special skills. (They are usually people with a gay or lesbian sibling or family member). The Board of Directors is also representative of the client-base. In many respects, GLASS is just like other Child Welfare agencies, but the key feature which makes this agency gay and lesbian-affirming is that it was conceived, designed, and developed by gay and lesbian Child Welfare professionals.

A central theme in the organizing of the GLASS program was that the agency is first and foremost a child welfare organization run by and for GLBT people. It is an organization which has as its central mission to work with GLBTQ adolescents and their families within the context of a child welfare environment.

The following section outlines concrete strategies for creating trans-affirming environments in other youth-serving agencies that may or may not be child welfare focused.

CONCRETE STRATEGIES

Hiring Supportive Employees

An organization that is responsive to the needs of transgendered youth must be staffed and administered by people who demonstrate a similar commitment to providing services that foster self-esteem and acceptance for transgendered youth. To achieve this, the organization must aim to hire open-minded, supportive employees, including openly gay, lesbian, bisexual, and transgender (GLBT) professionals. Organizations must communicate anti-discrimination policies in hiring, and must be honest about recruiting and maintaining GLBT employees. Hiring openly GLBT employees sends a clear message that the agency is demonstrating its commitment to transgendered youth.

Although hiring GLBT staff is critical, it should not be assumed that every GLBT person is knowledgeable about working with transgendered youth, or appropriate for working with them. All staff, regardless of sexual orientation or gender identification, should be assessed for their appropriateness in working with youth, and then educated about transgendered youth, the problems they experience in society, and how to effectively intervene with them. Hiring non-GLBT staff, who are comfortable with transgendered clients and open to being educated about working with this population, is also an essential part of this process.

With increasing openness about sexual and gender orientation, clients often ask employees about their sexual and gender orientation. One agency, Green Chimneys Children's Services, has encouraged staff to be open about their orientation, whatever their orientation happens to be. Ambiguity about staff's orientation leads to mistrust in the youth. Once staff are clear, residents stopped playing the guessing games and started to do the work that they had come to the agency for in the first place.

One of the most positive outcomes of recruiting openly GLBT staff reported by several of the agencies was that staff turnover was at an all time low rate. Being able to be employed in an accepting atmosphere is a great employee benefit for transgendered persons.

In-Service Training

In-service training, integrated into the overall training efforts of the organization, and not one-shot training deals, is critical in providing quality services to transgendered youth and families. As with all issues of diversity, integrating real-life case examples into the training sessions can make the educational process come alive for workers. Helping staff to identify appropriate language, bashing the common myths and stereotypes that most people have about transgendered persons, replacing the myths with accurate information about the population, and helping staff to create environments that suggest safety, are all good places to start. Training efforts should, however, be tailored to meet the individual needs of staff members from various disciplines.

Helping staff to identify resources in the community and to assess their own personal heterocentrism are also key factors in the training process. Use of videos and guest speakers–especially transgendered youth or their parents–can be particularly effective in getting the message across.

Transferring abstract information learned in training sessions into actual intervention techniques takes practice. Participation in a variety of experiential exercises assists staff members in beginning to develop a set of apt and unconstrained responses. Staff members in the training sessions should be intentionally exposed to situations that lead to self-reflection. For example, in one training focusing on the maladaptive coping responses that can be associated with hiding one's sexual or gender orientation, participants were asked at the start of the session to write their most personal secret on a slip of paper, to fold it, and to place it under the chair that they would be sitting on all day. Without ever being asked to share what they wrote, the message which is kept secret can be stressful and difficult. In ensuing discussion, attitudinal change and understanding of the consequences of secrecy often begin to evolve.

Providing staff at the training sessions with written information, resources, and other materials, insures that the educational process continues after the training session is finished. Training which includes on-going sessions and follow-up, and not one-shot deals, is the most constructive.

Welcoming Strategies

The creation of a physical environment that welcomes transgendered youth, families, and prospective employees is as significant as staff training. Again, these efforts do not need to cost a great deal of money. Evidence of an affirming environment signals acceptance and safety.

The organization's waiting room is probably the most important place to start this process. Reading materials, symbols, and signs that specifically spell out the organization's attitude about respect for all people will be noticed and will help clients, their families, and employment applicants feel welcomed.

Many agencies have posters hung in their waiting rooms that signal acceptance. Green Chimneys Children's Services has specifically developed nine colorful, gender neutral posters that announce a gay/lesbian or transgendered-affirming environment. The messages that these send are intentionally subtle. National transgendered organizations will also be able to provide youth-serving agencies with pamphlets and materials; others can be downloaded from the Internet.

The presence or lack of books focusing on transgendered issues also conveys important messages. Hundreds of transgendered-related books could also be purchased on-line using the services of either Amazon.com or BarnesandNoble.com

Integrated Policies and Public Information Materials

An organization's commitment to transgendered youth involves more than posters and books. Recognizing that the internal structure of the organization, by way of its policies and public information materials, may also need to be evaluated is critical (Frost & Egri, 1991). Training and educational efforts may assist staff in developing their competence in working with a service population, but policies and what the outside community knows about the organization may also need to be altered to effect real change (Bolman & Terrance, 1991; Brager & Holloway, 1978; Moss-Kanter, 1988).

Although transgendered persons have experienced greater acceptance and understanding in the past 30 years, many organizations may still actively discriminate against transgendered youth. In other cases, the organization's inattentiveness to the needs of transgendered youth will send a clear signal that they are not welcomed. A review of an organization's policies and public materials can assist the organization in consistently attempting to provide sensitive services to all youth.

Advocacy Efforts

Recognizing that the environment outside the organization is often actively hostile to transgendered youth, youth-serving agencies must also be committed to external change and advocacy efforts as well. This means participation in an advocacy campaign to end discriminatory language in contracts and in human services-related conferences. Affirming organizations must also be prepared to advocate for transgendered youth in community schools, in local adolescent treatment settings, and in families. Further, the organization's leaders must also be prepared to work to educate local and state politicians and funders about the needs of transgendered youth.

CONCLUSION

As the new century approaches, youth workers continue to play a critical role in developing young people. Youth work has historically had a cyclical interest in certain subjects: youth suicide, violence, substance abuse, and homelessness. All are worthwhile issues which require our best efforts, but the needs of transgendered youth should not be viewed as the "issue du jour" of youth work. Sexual orientation issues are too vital to continue to be overlooked. A particular transgendered client might trigger a plethora of attention at the time, only to fade from view when the next pressing issue presents itself. Dealing with transgendered youth issues in an intermittent manner is a mistake. Organizations must continue to develop diligence in training, assess their own ability or inability to respond to the needs of transgendered youth, and address new approaches to competent practice with these youth and their families. For an organization to be consistently sensitive to the needs of its clients, efforts to create affirming environments and to transform existing ones must be realized. If organizations are guided by the same principles that embrace diversity, and can translate these into concrete action, transgendered youth will be better served.

REFERENCES

Bolman, L., & Terrance, D. (1991). *Reframing organizations*. San Francisco: Jossey-Bass.

Brager, G., & Holloway, S. (1978). *Changing human service organizations: Politics and practice*. NY: Free Press.

Dutton, J.E. (1992). The making of organizational opportunities: An interpretive pathway to organizational change. *Research in Organizational Behavior, 15*, 195-226.

Feinberg, L. (1993). *Stone butch blues*. Ithaca, NY: Firebrand Books.

Frost, P. J., & Egri, C. P. (1991). The political process of innovation. *Research in Organizational Behavior, 13*, 229-295.

Gonsiorek, J. C. (1982). Organizational and staff problems in gay/lesbian mental health agencies. *Homosexuality and Psychotherapy, 7*(2/3), 193-208.

Greeley, G. (1994). Service organizations for gay and lesbian youth. In T. De Crescenzo (Ed.), *Helping gay and lesbian youth: New policies, new programs, new practice* (pp. 111-130). New York: Haworth Press.

Israel, G., & Tarver, D.E. (1997). *Transgender care*. Philadelphia: Temple University Press.

Kets de Vries, M. F. R., & Miller, D. (1984). *The neurotic organization*. NY: Harper Business.

Mallon, G. P. (1998). *We don't exactly get the welcome wagon: The experience of gay and lesbian adolescents in child welfare agencies.* New York: Columbia University Press.

Moss-Kanter, R. (1988). When a thousand flowers bloom: Structural, collective, and social conditions for innovation in organization. *Research in Organizational Behavior, 10,* 169-211.

Sawyer, D.A., & Woodlock, D.J. (1995). An organizational culture paradigm for effective residential treatment. *Administration and Policy in Mental Health, 22*(4), 437-446.

Scholinski, D. (1997). *The last time I wore a dress.* New York: Riverhead Books.

Schorr, L. B. with D. Schorr (1988). *Within our reach: Breaking the cycle of disadvantage.* New York: Doubleday.

Appendix A:
A Glossary of Transgendered Definitions

This glossary is intended to orient the reader to the more commonly used vocabulary in transgender literature and speech. Language is often a source of confusion and misinformation and as such, it is important that service providers have accurate definitions. Heterosexually oriented care providers are often unfamiliar and uncomfortable with the vernacular of the transgender culture. It should be recognized that, as with any sub-culture–particularly oppressed groups–there is a constantly changing argot. Usage may vary with generation, geographic region of the country, socioeconomic status, and cultural background.

Sex: The biological status as a female or male.

Sexual Identity: An individual's sense of self as male or female from the social and psychological perspective. Identity is the culturally informed process of expressing desires in a social role and with socially shared cultural practices within a social context.

Gender Identity: Refers to a person's innate sense of maleness or femaleness. Transgendered individuals report having experienced conflict over such gender assignment throughout childhood and adolescence.

Gender Role: The characteristics of an individual, which are culturally defined as masculine or feminine.

Sexual Orientation: The commonly accepted, scientific term for the direction of sexual attraction, emotional and/or physical attraction, and its expression. Examples of sexual orientation are: heterosexuality, homosexuality, and bisexuality.

[Haworth co-indexing entry note]: "Appendix A: A Glossary of Transgendered Definitions." Mallon, Gerald P. Co-published simultaneously in *Journal of Gay & Lesbian Social Services* (Harrington Park Press, an imprint of The Haworth Press, Inc.) Vol. 10, No. 3/4, 1999, pp. 143-145; and: *Social Services with Transgendered Youth* (ed: Gerald P. Mallon) Harrington Park Press, an imprint of The Haworth Press, Inc., 1999, pp. 143-145. Single or multiple copies of this article are available for a fee from The Haworth Document Delivery Service [1-800-342-9678, 9:00 a.m. - 5:00 p.m. (EST). E-mail address: getinfo@haworthpressinc.com].

Transgender: Transgender is an umbrella term encompassing the diversity of gender expression including drag queens and kings, bigenders, cross-dressers, transgenderists and transsexuals. These individuals, many of whom cluster together to form their own communities, are people who find their gender identity–the sense of themselves as male or female–in conflict with their anatomical gender.

Some transsexuals may live part time in their self-defined gender. Others desire to live fully in their self-identified gender.

Most of Western society continues to view the transgender experience as "abnormal." For many transgendered persons this results in secrecy, shame, depression, and fear. Such feelings can lead to increased isolation and the adoption of maladaptive coping mechanisms to deal with the stress of living in an environment, which not only expects compulsory heterosexuality, but conformity to mandatory gender roles as interpreted by Western society.

In recent years, some social work professionals have recognized that the needs of the transgendered community are similar, yet different from the needs of gay and lesbian persons with whom they are frequently united under the banner of sexual minority persons. In order to create greater acceptance and adaptedness to their inner feelings, transgendered persons have begun to create their own community support networks and organizations.

Gender Pronouns: He or She? How do I refer to this person? This is typically one of the first questions nontransgendered professionals and other interested people ask. The answer is: ask the person which pronoun he or she prefers.

MTF and FTM: These are acronyms that refer, respectively to "male to female" and "female to male" transitions. These designations reflect which direction of transition the person has taken.

Cross-Dressing: When a person dresses in the clothing of the opposite gender, i.e., males who wear traditionally female clothing, hairstyles, make-up, etc. Cross-dressing is sometimes referred to as gender nonconforming behavior.

Transvestite: Men or women who wear clothing usually worn by persons of the opposite gender. Most transvestites are heterosexual, mostly married men, who "cross-dress" in the privacy of their own homes, for sexual or psychological gratification. Transvestites are not to be confused with female impersonators. Female impersonators are men who earn a living by "cross-dressing" and performing in nightclubs.

Drag Kings/Queens: These persons are heterosexual or gay/lesbian and are usually performers. There are some gay men or lesbians who "cross-dress" in public; this is referred to as "being in drag" and these men are often referred to as "drag queens." Men who dress as women for performance; women who dress as men for performance. RuPaul is a drag queen, a gay man who dresses as a woman as entertainment.

Transsexuals: Are individuals who feel an overwhelming desire to permanently fulfill their lives as members of the opposite gender. Transsexuals most commonly experience the most acute effects of gender dysphoria. Many, though not all, opt for hormone therapy and genital reassignment surgery. These individuals can identify as heterosexual, gay or lesbian, or bisexual.

Intersexed or Hermaphrodite Individuals: Are those individuals with medically established physical or hormonal attributes of both male and female gender. When these conditions are detected at birth, these individuals are almost always assigned a gender solely on the basis of physical gender.

Persons on the Transgender Spectrum: Individuals who identify with any of the identities defined above, as transsexuals, drag kings/queens, transvestites, or cross dressers.

Spooked: Is a street-term for the moment when someone finds out that an individual is not biologically the gender that they were presenting.

Realness: Is a street-term that many youth use to remark on how authentic one appears to be.

Real-Life Test: Is an assessment term used to describe the period from the time a transsexual individual begins living in role to the time when she or he has been doing so long enough to be considered an appropriate candidate for genital reassignment surgery.

Appendix B:
A Guide to Staff Self-Awareness

One of the best ways of preparing to work with transgendered youth is to examine your own issues with respect to transgendered persons. The following is a guide describing first, the negative aspects of some youth workers' practice, followed by affirming approaches:

Negative Approaches

Assessment

- believes that transgendered identification is a disorder
- automatically attributes problems to gender identity
- fails to recognize heterocentrism or internalized homophobia
- assumes heterosexuality or homosexuality

Intervention

- irrelevantly focuses on sexual orientation rather than gender issues
- applies pressure to conform to biological gender orientation
- trivializes gender orientation experiences
- inappropriately transfers client upon client's disclosure

Identity

- does not understand gender identity development
- does not sufficiently take into account effects of internalized hatred

[Haworth co-indexing entry note]: "Appendix B: A Guide to Staff Self-Awareness." Mallon, Gerald P. Co-published simultaneously in *Journal of Gay & Lesbian Social Services* (Harrington Park Press, an imprint of The Haworth Press, Inc.) Vol. 10, No. 3/4, 1999, pp. 147-149; and: *Social Services with Transgendered Youth* (ed: Gerald P. Mallon) Harrington Park Press, an imprint of The Haworth Press, Inc., 1999, pp. 147-149. Single or multiple copies of this article are available for a fee from The Haworth Document Delivery Service [1-800-342-9678, 9:00 a.m. - 5:00 p.m. (EST). E-mail address: getinfo@haworthpressinc.com].

- underestimates possible consequences of coming out

Relationships

- underestimates importance of intimate relationships
- uses a heterosexual frame of reference

Family

- presumes transgendered client to be a poor parent
- is insensitive to prejudice toward families affected by gender identity issues

Youth Worker Expertise and Training

- lacks expertise and relies on client to educate the worker about the issues
- teaches inaccurate information or discriminates against transgendered trainees/colleagues

Exemplary Practice

Assessment

- understands that gender identity does not equal biological gender
- recognizes effects of societal gender conformity pressures
- recognizes that gender orientation is one of many attributes; does not assume it is necessarily the primary "problem"
- recognizes the unique concerns of transgendered youth of color

Intervention

- uses understanding of gender issues to guide therapy
- recognizes effects of one's own gender orientation, attitudes or lack of knowledge
- does not engage in therapy strategies to change sexual orientation or gender identity

Identity

- assists in development of positive trans-identity

Relationships and Family

- understands and validates diversity of relationships
- recognizes importance of extended families and families of creation
- recognizes effect of prejudice and discrimination on relationships and parenting
- recognizes that the family of origin may need education and support

Youth Worker Expertise and Education

- knows needs and treatment issues, and uses resources
- educates trainees/colleagues and actively counters negative stereotypes

Index

Abuse
    from family, 42,57-58,60,76
    physical, 78,97,99-100
    school-based, 10-11,25,43-45,62,
        78,97-98
    sexual, 60,62,96,99-100
    verbal, 42,70,72,135
Acceptance
    as practice approach, 45,77-78,
        97,101,139-140
    transsexuals' desire for, 91-93
Accident-proneness, 71
Accreditation standards, for Social
        Work schools, 7
Activists, transgendered, 9,63,118
Adaptive tasks
    in gender variant children, 51,68
    need for, 2,11,15,84,123
Adolescents
    case examples, 26-34
    comorbidity disorders, 20,24,
        36-38,40-41
    consent for treatment, 20-21,23,30
    ethical issues involving, 20-23,
        33-34
    gender identity disorder criteria,
        39-40
    maturity criteria, 21
    physical changes in,
        24-25,40-41,120
    psychological changes in, 24-25,
        40-41
    transitions of, 24-25,122
        female-to-male, 70-72
        male-to-female, 86-93
    treatment approaches, 19-20,23-26
Adults
    gender-conflicted, 52-53
    gender identity disorder criteria,
        39-40

    socialization systems for, 41-42
Advocates
    patients as, 84
    practitioners as, 45,57-58,76,
        134-140
Affirmation, positive, in practice,
        45,57-58,76,134-140
After-school programs, 44
Agencies. *See* Social service agencies
AIDS, in sex workers, 97
Alcohol abuse. *See* Substance abuse
American Academy of Child
        Psychiatry, 21
American Psychological Association,
        21-22
Androgynes, unification movement of,
        36
Anger, in children, 51,117
Anxiety
    during group work, 101-102
    in transgendered youth, 24,51,57,
        65,73,117
Attitudes
    negative. *See* Hostile environment
    nonjudgmental, importance of,
        14-15
Auto-castration, by adolescents, 41
Autonomy, for adolescents, 20,22-23,
        28,30
Aversion therapy, 9,54,56,61

Behavior therapy, 24,38,57
Behaviors, nonconforming at-risk. *See*
       also Sex workers
    of gender variant children,
        51-54,58,62,117
    of transgendered adolescents, 20,
        23-24,36-38,97
    of transsexual adolescents, 70-73,
        79,91

   151